The Gospel Corrupted

STILL HERE® Books by Kermit Zarley
Book 1: *The Third Day Bible Code* (2006)
Book 2: *Warrior from Heaven* (2009)
Book 3: *Moses Predicted COVID-19* (2020)
Book 4: *Bible Predicts Trump Fall* (2021)
Book 5: *The Late Great Plastic Empire* (forthcoming)

Other Books by Kermit Zarley
The Gospel (1987)
The Gospels Interwoven (1987)
Palestine Is Coming: The Revival of Ancient Philistia (1990)
The Restitution: Biblical Proof Jesus Is NOT God
(2008, title changed 2023)
Solving the Samaritan Riddle: Peter's Kingdom Keys Explain Spirit Baptism (2015)
The Gospel Corrupted: When Jesus Was Made God (2023)

The Gospel Corrupted
When Jesus Was Made God

Kermit Zarley

THE GOSPEL CORRUPTED: WHEN JESUS WAS MADE GOD

Copyright © 2023 by Kermit Zarley. All rights reserved. Except for brief quotations, no portion of this book may be reproduced in any form, stored in a retrieval system, or transmitted in any form or by any means—electronic, mechanical, photocopy, recording, or any other—without written permission of publisher or author. Contact him at kermitzarley.com.

Published by Kermit Zarley Enterprises.

Library of Congress Cataloging-in-Publication Data
Zarley, Kermit, 1941-
   The Gospel Corrupted: When Jesus Was Made God
     Bibliography: p.
     1. Jesus Christ—Person and offices. 2. Church Fathers—History. 3. Bible. N. T.—
     Theology. 4. Christianity—origin. I. Title.

Paperback: ISBN 978-1-7352591-7-8
E-Book: ISBN 978-1-7352591-8-5

Unless otherwise noted, all Scripture quotations are from the New Revised Standard Version of the Bible: UPDATED EDITION, marked (NRSVue), copyright © 1989, 1997, 2023 by the National Council of the Churches of Christ in the United States of America. Used by permission. All rights reserved worldwide.

Scripture quotations marked (KJV) are taken from the King James Version (KJV) of the Bible.

Scripture quotations marked (NASB) are taken from the New American Standard Bible*, Copyright© 1960, 1962, 1963, 1968, 1971, 1972, 1973, 1975, 1977, 1995 by The Lockman Foundation. Used by permission. www.Lockman.org.

Scripture quotations marked (NIV) are taken from the Holy Bible, New International Version*, NIV*. Copyright © 1973, 1978, 1984, 2011 by Biblica, Inc.™ Used by permission of Zondervan. All rights reserved worldwide. www.zondervan.com. The "NIV" and "New International Version" are trademarks registered in the United States Patent and Trademark Office by Biblica, Inc.™

Scripture quotations marked (ESV) are taken from ESV* Bible (The Holy Bible, English Standard Version*), copyright © 2001 by Crossway, a publishing ministry of Good News Publishers. Used by permission. All rights reserved.

Edited by Susanne Lakin
Cover design by Christy Eller

Contents

Abbreviations	vi
Preface	vii
Ch 1: My Christological Journey	1
Ch 2: What Is the Christian Gospel?	14
Ch 3: The Gospel According to Church Fathers	24
Ch 4: The Gospel According to Matthew, Mark, and Luke	35
Ch 5: The Gospel According to John	44
Ch 6: The Gospel According to the Acts of the Apostles	54
Ch 7: The Gospel According to Paul	64
Ch 8: Relations Between Three Monotheistic Religions	74
Ch 9: Did the Gospel Evolve and Did Jesus Know Who He Was?	80
Ch 10: Restitution at the Judgment	90
Works Cited	97
Author Index	98
Subject and Name Index	99
Scripture Index	102
The Real Jesus Tract	107
Books by Kermit Zarley	109

Abbreviations

1. General

BCE—before the Common Era	Gr.—Greek
c.—*circa*, about	Heb.—Hebrew
CE—Common Era	orig.—original
cf.—*confer*, compare	p., pp.—page, pages
ed(s).—editor(s), edition, edited by	rep.—reprint
esp.—especially	rev. ed.—revised edition
e.g.—*exempli gratia*, for example	tr.—translated
et al.—*et alii*, and others	v., vv.—verse, verses
etc.—*et cetera*, and so forth	vol(s).—volume(s)

2. Bible Versions, Bible

ESV	The Holy Bible, English Standard Version (2001)
KJV	King James Version (1611)
LXX	Septuagint (Gr. OT)—3rd c. BCE Greek translation of the Hebrew Bible
NASB	New American Standard Bible (orig. 1960; 1995)
NIV	The Holy Bible, New International Version (orig. 1978; 2011)
NRSVue	New Revised Standard Version Bible, Updated Edition (2021)
NT	New Testament
OT	Old Testament

Preface

Soon after I republished my large book with the title changed to *The Restitution: Biblical Proof Jesus Is Not God*, I thought of writing this little book, which is similar. Since I knew this genre well, I couldn't think of a book like I was envisioning. I then emailed some of my non-Trinitarian Christian friends who had authored books about it. I described my idea and asked if they knew of such a book. No one said "yes." And when I searched the internet to learn if such a book existed in English, I couldn't find anything that had a title anywhere near what I was thinking about. That surprised me even more. All of this caused me to decide that such a book was needed.

So, what is this book about? In it, I try to show that "the gospel," as set forth in the Bible's New Testament, consists of only a few essentials of Christian faith and that only these must be believed to receive God's salvation and thereby become a Christian. The book shows that church fathers later added to this original gospel by saying Jesus is God, God is three Persons, and people also must believe these propositions to be saved. Many scholars now agree that these were *additions* to the primitive, Christian gospel. I then claim that church fathers were not divinely authorized to *change the gospel*.

The same day that I conceived of this book, I pondered titling it *Church Fathers Changed the Gospel*. Five days later, I thought of substituting the word "Corrupted" for "Changed." I wondered if that is unfairly provocative. So, I prayed about it that evening. The next morning, I decided to read the credal statement produced by the Council of Chalcedon in 451. This decision had nothing to do with that prayer. I Googled "Council of Chalcedon statement." The first entry, ironically, was on R. C. Sproul's website for Legonier Ministries. There, I read the Chalcedonian Definition of Faith. It mentions people "daring to corrupt the mystery of the Lord's incarnation for us, and denying the title 'Theotokos' to the virgin." (Theotokos means "God-bearing." It refers to belief in Jesus's mother Mary as "mother of God" since Jesus was believed to be God.) This statement also mentions "those who attempt to corrupt the mystery of the incarnation, and who shamelessly pretend that He who was born of the holy Mary was a mere man."

That last clause refers to people like me! As I read the word "corrupt" in this Definition, not once but twice, I concluded it seemed God had answered my prayer by directing me to read this. I then decided to use "Corrupted" in my book title. I would take the word church fathers applied to people like me and throw it right back at them.

This book treats what can be a dense and complex subject. I have tried to make it as accessible as possible for a general readership. To do so, it has few footnotes. When I do cite authors, I usually appeal to leading Bible scholars, theologians, and historians.

Regarding this book's terminology, I often use the word "traditionalist" to refer to people who believe Jesus is God because some of them are not Trinitarian. And I usually describe their belief as "Jesus is God" rather than "deity of Christ" since "Jesus is God" is easier for common readers to understand. And I refrain from the notion of calling Jesus "divine" since traditionalist scholars who do so in their writings rarely define the term.

Finally, I view this book as a primer for *The Restitution*, which I sometimes quote herein. How do these two books compare? This book is personal, and it focuses on what the New Testament gospel is and how church fathers changed it. *The Restitution* is a 570-page book that is mostly a detailed analysis of the major, critical texts in the Bible, which traditionalists usually cite when asserting Jesus is God. In that book, I cite the written works of more than four hundred scholars. In this book, not so much.

Chapter 1
My Christological Journey[1]

Hello Church Fathers:[2]

I am writing to you about our common salvation in our Lord and Savior Jesus Christ. God, our Father Almighty, sent Jesus to redeem us flawed human beings from the slave market of sin by means of his atoning death on the cross. God proved it by raising Jesus from the dead. For us who have sincerely believed this, God lifted us up to experience an abundant life now and eternal life in his future, glorious kingdom to come. Amen!

I'm sure that many of you church fathers did many good and wonderful deeds in your lives for which you will be greatly honored at the future judgment to be conducted by God through his Christ. And for your righteous acts you will be immensely rewarded beyond imagination so that you will enjoy the fruits of your labor for all eternity.

Nevertheless, I regret to inform you that I have a complaint against some of you. You Nicene church fathers claimed that Jesus is God, declaring in your Nicene Creed that Jesus is "very God of very God" (Gk. *alethinon theon*), meaning "true God of true God," and you made this dictum a faith requirement for salvation. Yet this notion does not appear anywhere in the New Testament gospel. Also, you boldly declared in this creed that dissenters of this proposition "are condemned by the catholic and apostolic Church." And nearly all Christians ever since have approved of these declarations.

Moreover, you Nicene and post-Nicene fathers condemned such dissenters no matter what else they believed about Jesus or whether they lived in obedience to his teachings. In this requirement, that people must believe Jesus is God to be saved, you *added* to the unadulterated and pure gospel of the Lord Jesus without his authorization.

---

[1] For more, see a series of twelve posts entitled "My Christological Journey" at Kermit Zarley Blog hosted by Patheos.com. In the menu, click "Archives" and scroll to October 22, 2018, for the first post.

[2] According to the authoritative *The SBL Handbook of Style: For Biblical Studies and Related Disciplines*, 2nd ed. (p. 39), the expression "church father(s)" is no longer supposed to be capitalized.

For you Nicene and post-Nicene fathers, and those Christians who have accepted these bold proclamations of yours, in this little book I will examine the Holy Scriptures to show that *you changed the gospel* of our Lord Jesus Christ. But, first, I will relate a little about my spiritual and theological journey to show where I'm coming from.

My Being Born Again

I did not grow up in a religious home. Yet, from age five, I attended Sunday school regularly. One spring day in 1954, when I was thirteen years old, I believed in Jesus and became a born-again Christian. My Sunday school teacher led me in private prayer to invite Jesus Christ into my life as "my Lord and Savior." For Jesus to be my living Savior meant that I believed he died on the cross for my sins and rose from the dead. For him to be my Lord meant that I would try to make him master of my life. *This is the gospel.*

But it was not until I went to college, at eighteen years of age, that I really began to learn the Bible and Christian theology. The pastor of my independent Bible church most zealously taught the Bible and much theology. It included the church doctrine of the Trinity, that God is one essence existing as three coequal and coeternal Persons: Father, Son (Jesus), and Holy Spirit. I also learned from him the hypostatic union of Christ—that Jesus is both man and God by having a human nature and a divine nature. And I was taught that Jesus always spoke and acted according to one of his two natures. My pastor taught these things because you church fathers made these determinations in your ecumenical councils in the 4th and 5th centuries and enshrined them in your creeds. From then on, I was a Trinitarian Christian who always attended Trinitarian churches.

My Moment of Christological Enlightenment

Then, in 1980, twenty years after I was taught the doctrine of the Trinity and its corollary, the hypostatic union of Christ, I was sitting in my study room in my home, reading my Bible. I had never questioned this teaching. I was reading Jesus's Olivet Discourse in Matthew 24—25 in my New American Standard Bible,[3] which I knew well. I came to Jesus's saying in Matthew 24:36 in which he says of his second coming, "But of that day and hour no one knows, not even the angels of heaven,

---

[3] Dallas Theological Seminary gave me this Bible for being a regular donor to that school.

nor the Son, but the Father alone." Suddenly, this statement caught my attention like never before. As I pondered it and what I had been taught about it, I grew disturbed. Then, I blurted out loud to myself these exact words: "*What! That makes Jesus look like a liar. He said he didn't know, but he really did know because he is God.*" What did I mean?

I was referring to the Trinity and the hypostatic union. I had been taught that Jesus said this in his human nature even though he really knew in his divine nature the time of his second coming. I thought some more about this seeming incongruity wherein Jesus appeared to be a liar. Then I said out loud to myself again softly, with a firm and solemn conviction, "I *will* stand on the integrity of Jesus. I *must* look into this."

I think that is the biggest understatement of my life! And I knew that questioning the core teaching of Christianity could have serious consequences for me ecclesiastically, socially, and ministerially. Yet, all my adult life my foremost desire had been to *know God's truth*. I began to wonder if church fathers could have gotten this wrong.

My Christological Research Begins

I became very devoted to studying whether Jesus is God. I first asked myself, "How should I begin this study?" I answered, "No one knows better who Jesus was than Jesus!" So, I decided that I needed to examine all of Jesus's sayings in the four gospels of the New Testament. I would look only for any statement in which he expressly declared, or even obscurely hinted, that he is God. And I thought the easiest way to do this would be to get a so-called "red-letter Bible." It has all of Jesus's sayings in red print. So, I purchased a red-letter New Testament from a Christian bookstore. Upon reading only the red words, *I discovered to my great surprise that Jesus never said he was God.* I already knew of his saying in John 10:30: "I and the Father are one." Many Trinitarians claimed this means Jesus and God the Father share the same essence, which is divine, so that both are God. I then said out loud to myself about this text, "If that is all they've got, I think I'm on the right track!" (Yeah, I sometimes talk to myself.)

About two years after I began this study, I was certain Jesus did not say he was God. It took me a few more years to abandon belief that Jesus had a lesser deity/divinity than that of God the Father. When I learned in the late 1980s that John 1:1c and 20:28 do not say Jesus is God, I have been certain ever since that the Bible does not say Jesus is God. I still clung for a while to the belief that Jesus preexisted. But I became certain in the mid-1990s that he didn't. So, it took me fifteen years of study to decide that *the Bible does not say Jesus was or is God or that he literally preexisted*. The risen Jesus was and still is a human being as God had intended humans to be when he created them.

I decided Jesus is not God at a most inopportune moment in my life—at 3:00 AM Sunday morning on June 20, 1982. I was about to play my final round in the U.S. Open at Pebble Beach Golf Course, my favorite tournament and my favorite golf course. (Tom Watson won.) On Friday, I had made the 36-hole cut by two strokes with a score of 149. In the third round, I shot a three-under-par 69 that moved me into position to have a respectably good tournament, maybe finish in the top-ten. But that Sunday, I played poorly and shot 78 to finish 39th, tied with stars Tom Weiskopf, Hale Irwin, and Curtis Strange. Irwin and Strange had won five U.S. Opens between them.

I had been looking forward to this tournament with much anticipation. Ten years prior, in June, 1972, I had a good chance to win it on this same golf course. It had always been my #1 dream in golf to win the U.S. Open. I was leading the tournament during the last round with twelve holes to play, one stroke ahead of Jack Nicklaus, who eventually won. From there I floundered miserably, shooting 79 to finish 6th.

About that last round in the U.S. Open in 1982, I should have gone to sleep hours earlier. But I was staying in a private home of a Christian couple, and the bedroom I was in had a theological library. I returned every day from the golf course to read books into the night. I deeply immersed myself in learning about Jesus's identity. That library had the eight-volume set of Lewis Sperry Chafer's *Systematic Theology*. He was the founder of Dallas Theological Seminary to which I was connected. In reading Chafer's arguments and others about Jesus's identity and the Trinity, I thought they were unconvincing.

Then, with much prayer and trepidation, I decided tentatively that the Bible does not say Jesus is God. I already was sure that *Jesus didn't say he was God*. And because of that I decided tentatively that *Jesus didn't think he was God*. These two beliefs about Jesus's identity then became my main arguments when I talked to others about this.

For me, the bottom line was this: Will I believe what Jesus says about who he is, or will I believe what the church says about it, which came from church fathers? The answer was a no-brainer: *I will believe what Jesus says about who he is, come hell or high water!* Since he did not say he was God, I will not believe he is God. Yet, I still wanted to talk to some experts about this most important subject.

Talking to Professors about Who Jesus Is

And I did. I immediately told my friend Jim Hiskey. (In 1965, he imparted the idea to me and his brother, my close friend Babe Hiskey, to start a Bible study on the PGA Tour. We did that year.) That summer in 1982, I was about to end my full-time career on the regular PGA Tour. I was considering Jim's invitation to work as an associate with him in The Fellowship (which I did the rest of the 1980s). But Jim was alarmed at my christological change. I was not surprised. He asked me to talk to three theology professors about it, whom he would choose. I accepted.

Jim first arranged for us and Dr. Ed Clowney, president of Westminster Seminary in Philadelphia, to play a round of golf together at Washington Golf Club in DC. After that, we had lunch in the clubhouse. Ed and I then discussed my change in Christology.

The next encounter was with R. C. Sproul. I skipped a PGA Tour tournament that summer, drove my family to Legonier, and we stayed at Sproul's Legonier Conference Center. R. C. and I then spent almost an entire day in his house discussing Christology.

I had been to nearby Latrobe as a guest of Arnold Palmer to tour his first house. He made it into a museum full of all his golf clubs and other equipment he used in his career. As for R. C., he required that we take periodic breaks from our discussion into his backyard so he could swing his golf club, and I would give him a golf swing lesson.

The third person was James Houston, president of Regents College in Vancouver, British Columbia. But this discussion only lasted about twenty minutes on the phone.

All three men reported back to Jim, giving me "a clean bill of spiritual health." Yet, I wanted mostly to talk about this with one of my mentors—Dr. S. Lewis Johnson Jr. of Dallas Theological Seminary.[4] He had guided me in writing my first book, and he wrote the foreword for it. The first time we talked about this was for six hours in his house. Lewis warned me, "If you keep believing this way, *you are not a Christian!*"

Johnson knew his theology well. I had listened to hundreds of hours of his Bible teaching tapes, including about 150 hours of his systematic theology that he also taught at the seminary. And I took voluminous notes. Plus, I had gotten him as guest speaker for two years at our annual PGA Tour Bible Conference that we held for three days at

---

[4] Johnson was a member of the translation committee of the New International Version of the Bible.

the beginning of the year. After Dr. Johnson and I had one more long talk about this subject, he would have nothing to do with me anymore. He used to write letters to me. I was heartbroken but, again, not surprised. I knew what I was getting into, that my departure from Trinitarianism and thus traditional Christology would result in me losing some dear Christian friends.

Two Final Obstacles to My Christological Research

After I tentatively decided in 1982 that I did not believe the Bible says Jesus is God, I was about 90 percent sure about it. There remained two brief verses in the New Testament that I called "obstacles" to my being certain. Both are in the Gospel of John: verses 1:1c and 20:28. The traditional translation of John 1:1c is "and the Word was God." Comparing this with what verse 14 says, "and the Word became flesh," which refers to Jesus, it implied to me that Jesus was God. And John 20:28 is about Doubting Thomas seeing and hearing the risen Jesus speak to him and exclaiming, "My Lord and my God!" But in the late 1980s, I got answers to my questions about these two texts.

I lived in metro-Houston, Texas. I sometimes drove to Dallas to study at DTS's Mosher Library. One day I asked the librarian, Marvin Hunn, whom I knew, if he knew of any notable scholar who claimed John 1:1c in the Greek text does not mean Jesus is God. Marvin replied, "Yes—Philip Harner." He directed me to Harner's article about this in a 1973 issue of the premier theological periodical—*Journal of Biblical Literature*.[5] I read it and thought Harner was right. His main issue regards how the anarthrous *theos* in John 1:1c should be treated since it's a grammatical issue. Harner recommended the New English Bible translation of it—"and what God was, the Word was." This rendering does not say "the Word was God" or indicate Jesus *was* God. It merely says Jesus was *like* God, presumably in character.

Also, about this time I was reading Rudolf Bultmann's commentary on the Gospel of John. Many liberal scholars had regarded him as the greatest New Testament scholar of the twentieth century. I noticed at Thomas's confession in John 20:28[6] that Bultmann cited for comparison the author's previous narration of

---

[5] Philip B. Harner, "Qualitative Anarthrous Predicate Nouns: Mark 15:39 and John 1:1," *Journal of Biblical Literature* 92 (1973): 75–87.

[6] Rudolf Bultmann, *The Gospel of John: A Commentary* (Westminster John Knox, 1971), 695.

a conversation that Jesus had with Thomas and Philip, recorded in John 14:5–11. Thomas started this conversation. Philip then said to Jesus, "'Lord, show us the Father, and we will be satisfied.' Jesus said to him ... 'Whoever has seen me has seen the Father'" (vv. 8–9). Did Jesus mean he was God the Father? No! He explained, saying it twice, "I am in the Father and the Father is in me" (vv. 10–11). Scholars call this "the mutual indwelling." I was surprised Bultmann didn't treat this text. I decided when Thomas later said to the risen Jesus, "My God," he meant what Jesus taught him days earlier, that *God the Father indwells Jesus*. The doubting apostle then realized the God indwelling Jesus had raised him from the dead.

I now had answers to the two biblical texts that had been obstacles preventing me from being certain that the Bible does not identify Jesus as God. Yet I still thought Jesus preexisted. I didn't think that meant he was God. Some Jewish rabbis believed one or more Bible heroes, such as Elijah or Moses, preexisted or went to heaven and returned, yet they did not think that required believing that they were God/gods.

It was not until 1994–1995 that I became certain that the Bible does not say Jesus literally preexisted. For example, Jesus said in his sermon in John 6, "I am the bread that came down from heaven" (v. 41). Then he said of himself, "Unless you eat the flesh of the Son of Man, and drink his blood, you have no life in you" (v. 53). He surely meant the bread, flesh, and blood metaphorically. Why? It would be inconsistent for Jesus to mean he literally "came down from heaven," thus preexisted, but intend his flesh and blood metaphorically. Thus, Jesus likely did not mean he literally came from heaven.

So, after fifteen years of much in-depth study, from 1980 to 1995, I was sure that the Bible does not say Jesus was or is God or that he literally preexisted.

The Depth of My Christological Research

I worked very hard at this study. My friend Dr. Dale Allison read the manuscript in late 2008 and critiqued it. I incorporated most of his suggestions. He wrote, "the 'God was in Christ' proposal is sensible. ... it merits discussion. You've done a lot of work."

I estimate that in the twenty-eight years after I began this research, I read about a thousand books on Jesus's identity. Obtaining them was not an easy task. As a layman, I did not have access to theological books as scholars and theologians usually do. I had to first learn who were distinguished scholars who wrote on this subject—whether Jesus is God.

Some of these books I purchased and added to my theological library in my study room. I had to obtain most of them through the interlibrary loan system. All of this took a huge amount of time and effort. Plus, I'm a slow reader. But I usually take notes. So, I began developing a sizable filing system wherein I kept my notes from this study.

Reading books consisted of only half or less of my research. The most important part was visiting theological libraries, usually at seminaries, many of them throughout the US, and scouring thousands of Bible commentaries. I read what they say about the critical texts in the Bible as to whether Jesus is God. I decided there are about forty or fifty such texts. But, after more study, I learned there are about nine major texts in the New Testament that distinguished scholars cite to support the view that Jesus is "God," which is *theos* in the Greek New Testament. They are as follows: John 1:1c; 1:18; 20:28; Romans 9:5; 2 Thessalonians 1:12; Titus 2:13; Hebrews 1:8; 2 Peter 1:1; and 1 John 5:20.

I was surprised to learn that *most of these major texts have some grammatical issue*. It is partly because ancient languages, such as Koine Greek of the New Testament, did not have space between words, upper and lower case, or even punctuation. So most modern Bible versions have alternate readings for these texts. One reading says Jesus is God, and the other reading does not. And linguists sometimes disagree on whether there was a grammatical rule in antiquity that affects how these texts should be translated.

Evangelistic messages in the New Testament are the gospel. And they are easy to comprehend. Therefore, scholars do not disagree on what they say. I decided those and explanations of the gospel (Gr. *euangelion*) should be distinguished from the rest of the New Testament, like putting Jesus's words in red. Why? I discovered that *all nine of those major, theos texts do not appear in any evangelistic messages or explanations of the gospel in the New Testament.* Church fathers inserted their misunderstanding of those grammatically difficult texts into the gospel.

My Lack of Credentials to Investigate Christology

Since I am a layman, thus lacking scholarly credentials, and I've questioned these declarations of church fathers, several people have said to me sarcastically, "Who do you think you are?" They insinuate I am an arrogant fool to question an important teaching of church fathers that has been affirmed through the centuries by so many theologians and Bible scholars more qualified than I am to so scrutinize. Yet, that is an *ad hominem* argument that detracts from the issues. Nevertheless, I will briefly address it here.

It just so happened that I chose to be a professional golfer for my life's work. Yet, I proved my intellectual ability in college by graduating with an academic honor. And some scholars who know me and have read some of my writings have acknowledged that I possess the intellectual capacity to have chosen the path in life they took that requires a PhD. (North Park University awarded me an honorary PhD due to my writings.)

Besides, most Christians are aware that Jesus was a common laborer before he became an itinerant preacher. So he was not trained by a professional elite to become a rabbi (though I endorse higher education). And when Jesus chose his twelve apostles, he did not select them from the Sanhedrin or the two theological schools in Jerusalem—the school of Hillel and the school of Shammai. Those apostles had no religious credentials. Andrew, Peter, James, and John were commercial fishermen. And Matthew was a tax collector. Plus, we read that the religious rulers at Jerusalem "saw the boldness of Peter and John and realized that they were uneducated and ordinary men" (Acts 4:13).

My change in christological belief may have happened partially because I am naturally an inquisitive person. In fact, I can irritate people with my habit of asking questions. So I try to not be too overbearing with that. Yet, I also believe in practicing what Jesus said in the Sermon on the Mount: "Ask, and it will be given to you; search, and you will find; knock, and the door will be opened for you" (Matthew 7:7).

Ever since college, the foremost prayer of my life has been, "Father, please teach me your truth." And sometimes I would add, "Lord, if I believe something wrong about your truth, please show me." I believe I had my moment of christological enlightenment while reading Matthew 24:36 because God answered this persistent prayer.

Free to Investigate

Also, since I was a professional golfer, my finances didn't depend on my theology. That helped free me to think more critically about all that I believe. But for many church pastors and some theology professors or the like, I don't think they are that free. Their theology can affect their finances. For them to believe as I do—that Jesus is Savior and Lord but not God and admit this publicly—it might get them fired! It could substantially reduce their incomes. And they might even find it difficult to gain future employment. Because of this, maybe I've been more qualified than most to look at this objectively. Maybe that's why the chairman of the board of a large corporation once told me while we were playing golf in a Senior Tour pro-am, "I would *never* read a theological book written by a scholar, but I might read one written by you."

And what about those church fathers who attended those ecumenical councils? They had to subscribe to the creeds that declared Jesus is God and God is three Persons. What would have happened to them if they had not subscribed to those creeds? Arius and his two bishop friends refused to sign the Nicene Creed. So Emperor Constantine exiled them from the empire. That harmed them more than losing a job and income.

I suspect some of those bishops were not convinced Jesus was fully God, but they subscribed to the creed to avoid persecution. If so, that reminds me of a comparable situation in the Bible. We read of Jesus, "Many even of the authorities believed in him. But because of the Pharisees they did not confess it, for fear that they would be put out of the synagogue; for they loved human glory more than the glory that comes from God" (John 12:42–43).

Now, all Christian theology should be decided according to what the Bible says. I don't trash creeds, since even the Bible has some brief credal statements. But post-apostolic creeds ought not be regarded as God-inspired to the extent the Bible is. Thus, church creeds should be scrutinized in comparison to the Bible. For the apostle Paul wrote, "All scripture is inspired by God" (2 Timothy 3:16).

Some church officials have advised people in the pew to believe what is preached in the pulpit about this and not investigate it for themselves, saying it is too complex for them to understand. On the contrary, I state in *The Restitution* (p. 5),

> Widely esteemed Roman Catholic NT scholar R. E. Brown well explains, "Christian believers whose spiritual lives should be shaped by the Master, if they have not wrestled in some mature way with the identity of Jesus, are in danger of constructing a fictional Jesus ... most people answer the question of the identity of Jesus without any real struggle to gain precision about what the NT says. ... Christology is so important an issue for religious adherence that one should not express judgments without seriously looking at the evidence."[7]

---

[7] Raymond E. Brown, *An Introduction to New Testament Christology* (New York:

The day after I wrote the above in this subhead, I read what Bill Ackman had just tweeted the day before about insight often coming from those who lacked credentials. Billionaire Ackman is one of the most successful investors on Wall Street. He is also the CEO of Pershing Square Capital. He posted on his Twitter account on June 18, 2023:

> I have learned from experience that the experts, the government, and conventional wisdom are often wrong. ... It is often the outlier with no experience in a field that challenges the status quo, that makes the important discovery, that has the unique insight, or creates the transformational innovation. ... When you are part of the establishment, it is hard to challenge the conventional wisdom. You are incentivized not to. And when your economic livelihood can be threatened by an alternative point of view or a new innovation, you are less likely to believe it or its viability.

I think that fits me to a tee, (golf pun intended). As I said, my living as a pro golfer has never depended on my theology, whereas for most Christian ministers it does.

Sometime after I began this study, I started writing a book about my findings. In 2008, twenty-eight years after I began this study, I self-published a six-hundred-page tome as my *magnum opus* entitled *The Restitution of Jesus Christ*. (I republished it in 2023 with a new title, *The Restitution: Biblical Proof Jesus Is Not God*.) In this book, I cite more than four hundred authors. Most of them are distinguished Bible scholars who excel in their specialized fields of study. The book begins with an introduction. Then it has one hundred pages of history about the development of church Christology. The rest of the book is a detailed examination of those Bible texts traditionalists cite to support their viewpoint that Jesus is God.

Conclusion

To sum up my research, I learned three things in the New Testament that caused me to no longer believe Jesus is God or the church doctrine of the Trinity. Here they are: (1) Jesus never says he is God, (2) Jesus's apostles never identify him as God in their evangelistic messages while preaching the gospel, and (3) most of the few Bible texts that Trinitarians cite to support their view that Jesus

---

Paulist, 1994), vi, 10–11.

is God have grammatical difficulties, causing Bible versions to vary in translating them.

Getting back to my complaint, you church fathers are telling me that I'm not a believer in Jesus, that I'm not a born-again Christian, that I'm a condemned heretic? In *The Restitution*, I displayed an irenic spirit, following the apostle Paul's instruction of practicing the "meekness and gentleness of Christ" (2 Corinthians 10:1). Yet, Paul also adds of himself and his ministry associates, "We destroy arguments and every proud obstacle raised up against the knowledge of God" (vv. 5–6). You church fathers, in your creeds you raised up a proud obstacle against the knowledge of God by declaring Jesus is God. And you asserted that if people do not believe this they are condemned. You have no support whatsoever from the New Testament for these bold assertions.

It is one thing to claim that Jesus is God. But it is quite another thing to make this precept a necessary belief for salvation. *That is adding to the gospel*! That is what irks me—changing the gospel that Jesus's apostles gave to the church. To those church fathers who are responsible for this unwarranted addition, and to those who follow them by saying people like me are not Christians, I declare to you, "No more Mr. Nice Guy!"

I had a good reputation with a public profile. I was helping to bring Christianity to American professional sports by cofounding and leading the PGA Tour Bible Study. But in the last forty years, I have lost more than half of my Christian friends, most of them in ministry. Many have accused me of being a heretic and thus a non-Christian due to what you church fathers did. I ignored their accusations, taking a spiritually noncombative stance in what I call "layin' low." I went thirty years being publicly silent about this.

I believe God called me to endure this rejection. The apostle Peter writes about this by saying, "For to this you have been called, because Christ also suffered for you, leaving you an example, so that you should follow in his steps" (1 Peter 2:21). I was sort of like Jesus about this, who, "like a sheep that before its shearers is silent, so he did not open his mouth" (Isaiah 53:7). But now I think it's time for me to speak boldly, to show that church fathers got this wrong. It's time for me to be like John the Baptist!

One time on the PGA Tour, I was paired with the Super Mex, Lee Trevino, in the Houston Open. There had been times when I tried to share the gospel with him. When we finished this round, Lee said to the media, "It's tough playin' on these bumpy greens out there." As I stood nearby, listening, Lee then pointed his finger at me with a gleam in his eye and added, "But it's *double-tough* playin' with John the Baptist."

So, starting with this little book, I'm going on the offensive like John the Baptist did. (Not physically, but verbally, because I abhor violence.) I'm takin' it to ya', folks! The gloves are off. Here goes: *Church Fathers Corrupted the Gospel*!

Chapter 2
What Is the Christian Gospel?

Christianity has been the largest religion in the world for the past 1,700 years. Its success is attributed to its "gospel." The Christian gospel is a message of glad tidings that brings great joy to people. This message is that God Almighty will forgive sinners of their sins, reconcile them to himself, and give them eternal life to live forever in his kingdom if they sincerely believe in the one whom he has sent—Jesus of Nazareth. But what must people believe about Jesus to be forgiven and thereby inherit eternal life? That is like asking, what is the Christian gospel? That is what this little book is about.

Some Christians have thought "the gospel" refers to all Christian doctrine. But I think a close examination of this term as it appears in the Bible reveals that it refers to a narrower message that contains only a few elements that are essential to believe to receive God's salvation and thereby live forever.

The Meaning of the Gospel in the Old Testament

The Bible's concept of "the gospel" appears first in the Old Testament. In its Hebrew text, the noun *besora* appears, which means "gospel," but it occurs seldom and only in a nonreligious context. In contrast, the verb *basar* occurs occasionally and always in a religious context. It is often translated "proclaim the good news" or the like.

The prophet Isaiah is known for proclaiming *basar*, meaning "good tidings." He relates, "Get you up to a high mountain, O Zion, herald of good tidings; lift up your voice with strength, O Jerusalem, herald of good tidings, lift it up, do not fear; say to the cities of Judah, 'Here is your God!' See, the Lord God comes with might, and his arm rules for him" (Isaiah 40:9–10). So, *mebaseret* appears twice in this Hebrew text to mean "one bringing good news." It indicates God reigns supreme over his chosen nation, Israel. The word *arm* is used as a metaphor that refers to Messiah as a warrior-king (cf. Luke 1:51). Since Jesus is this Messiah, this text refers to his second coming. The words "Here is your God" indicates God's strength will then be displayed in all its glory in Jesus.

Isaiah 52:7–10 is an oracle like Isaiah 40:1–11. The seer begins, "How beautiful upon the mountains are the feet of the messenger who announces peace, who brings good news, who announces salvation, who says to Zion, 'Your God reigns'" (Isaiah 52:7). Isaiah concludes, "The LORD has bared his holy arm before the eyes of all the nations, and all the ends of the earth shall see the salvation of our God" (v. 10). God baring his strong arm, again, refers to Messiah Jesus's second coming at the end of the age.

Isaiah soon proclaims again about Messiah Jesus, "Who has believed what we have heard? And to whom has the arm of the LORD been revealed?" (Isaiah 53:1). The rest of Isaiah 53 is an amazing prophecy about Jesus as God's righteous servant who will suffer for the sins of others, culminating in his martyr death and resurrection.

Isaiah also presents Jesus's public ministry by putting in his mouth the following, "The spirit of the Lord God is upon me, because the LORD has anointed me; he has sent me to bring good news to the oppressed, to bind up the broken hearted, to proclaim liberty to the captives, and release to the prisoners, to proclaim the year of the LORD's favor, and the day of vengeance of our God" (Isaiah 61:1–2). Here, as in Isaiah 40:9 and 52:7, *basar* in the Hebrew text means "good news." Although these proclamations of Isaiah may apply to his time, "the day of vengeance" refers especially to Jesus's second coming. Then God will act like no other time in exercising vengeance upon his enemies.

In the Old Testament, the concept of the kingdom of God, meaning God's reign, is most prominent in the apocalyptic book of Daniel. Babylonian King Nebuchadnezzar's dream recorded in Daniel 2 is a prophecy about four future world empires that are instantly destroyed by the kingdom of God coming from heaven to fill the whole earth and last forever. Daniel 7:13–14 portrays a royal scene in heaven in which Jesus, as "one like a son of man," is presented before God at the end of the age to receive this kingdom.

The Meaning of the Gospel in the New Testament

The most important message in the New Testament about Christian faith is "the gospel." The English word *gospel* combines the Old English word *god*, meaning "good," and *spell*, meaning "talk." So *gospel* meant "good talk" or "good news."

In English Bibles, the New Testament often mentions "gospel" or "good news." Both translate the noun *euangelion* in the Greek text.

Its etymology is that *eu* means "well" or "good" and *angello*—from which we derive our English word *angel*—means "to announce." So, *euangelion* means a message of "good news" or "good tidings."

This Greek word *euangelion* was commonly used in the Hellenistic world in the time of Jesus. Greeks had used it to designate a ritual sacrifice of thanks dedicated to the gods. It came to be applied to important events, such as the birth date of a Caesar to signify that he was destined to be a benefactor to the Roman Empire, thus "good news."

In the Greek New Testament, *euangelion* often stands alone as a noun. But it can be in the genitive case, often translated "the gospel of the kingdom," "the gospel of God," or "the gospel of Christ." And the Greek text sometimes has the verb *euangelizomai*. It usually is translated in English Bibles "preach the gospel" or "proclaim the good news." Also, *euangelion* occurs in the Greek text about sixty times in the apostle Paul's letters. For instance, he quotes both Isaiah 52:7 and 53:1, previously cited, in Romans 10:15–16.

"Good news" first appears in the New Testament, in which an angel proclaims the births of John the Baptist and Jesus (Luke 1:19; 2:10). Gabriel says to Mary, "You will name him Jesus. He will be great ... and the Lord God will give him the throne of his ancestor David. He will reign over the house of Jacob forever, and of his kingdom there will be no end" (Luke 1:31–33). So this good news is about Jesus and his kingdom.

The Gospel of Mark begins, "The beginning of the good news of Jesus Christ" (Mark 1:1). Again, "good news" translates *euangelion* in the Greek text. English Bibles often translate it "gospel." Mark also relates, "Jesus came to Galilee proclaiming the good news of God and saying, 'The time is fulfilled, and the kingdom of God has come near; repent, and believe in the good news'" (vv. 14–15). In both cases, *euangelion* in the Greek text is translated "good news." The first Gentile believers in Jesus often used the word *euangelion* to refer to their salvation message they proclaimed to the world.

Scholars claim that the four gospels of the New Testament originally did not have titles and that they were added in about the late second century CE. The Greek word *euangelion* is used in those titles in a different sense than it is used in the Greek New Testament, that is, to indicate a certain type of book. The Greek word *kata*, which means "according to," was added in these titles to indicate that the content of each of these books represents the author's account of the good news about Jesus of Nazareth.

The Content of the Original Christian Gospel

Since *gospel* means "good news," what is the good news? *The Christian gospel is the proclamation that God has brought forgiveness of sins, and thus salvation, to humankind through Jesus Christ.* It is both personal and universal. Since *Christ* means Messiah, a king, this gospel is about the kingdom that God will give Jesus and, through him, God's chosen nation Israel, and all nations will be blessed by it. So, in its original New Testament form, *gospel* is that which was proclaimed, not a written book.

For example, the Gospel of Luke informs that when Jesus was born in Bethlehem, an angel appeared to nearby shepherds at night. He announced to them, "I am bringing you good news of great joy for all the people; to you is born this day in the city of David a Savior, who is the Messiah, the Lord" (Luke 2:10–11). The phrase, "I am bringing to you good news," translates *hymin euangelizomai* in the Greek text. It can be rendered literally: "I evangelize you."

Jesus came preaching the gospel to Israel. For instance, at the synagogue in his hometown of Nazareth, Jesus read from Isaiah the prophet, "The Spirit of the Lord is upon me, because he has anointed me to bring good news to the poor, he has sent me to proclaim release to the captives, and recovery of sight to the blind" (Luke 4:18). The words "bring good news" are the translation of *euangelisasthai* in the Greek text. It also can be translated "evangelize." The King James Version renders it "preach the gospel."

The text Jesus read was Isaiah 61:1. He applied it to himself, saying, "Today this scripture has been fulfilled in your hearing" (Luke 4:21). Isaiah's phrase, "bring good news," translates *le-basar* in the Hebrew Bible. The Septuagint (the Greek translation of the Hebrew Bible) has *euangelisasthai*, the same word in the Greek text of Luke 4:18.

Therefore, Jesus was the original bringer of good news. He came preaching his gospel to Israel, thereby evangelizing the nation. Matthew says Jesus was "teaching in their synagogues and proclaiming the good news of the kingdom and curing every disease and every sickness" (Matthew 4:23; 9:35). He was calling Jews to repent of their sins toward God and believe in God's kingdom promised to them in their Scriptures.

Jesus ministered only among Jews because God's plan was to give the nation of Israel every opportunity to repent and thereby receive the promised kingdom. For, he said, "I was sent only to the lost sheep of the house of Israel" (Matthew 15:24). Likewise, Jesus sent his disciples to evangelize, telling them, "Go nowhere among the Gentiles ... As you go, proclaim the good news, 'The kingdom of heaven has come near'" (10:5, 7).

After Jesus died, was entombed, and rose from the dead, the gospel that he had preached became more multifaceted. It now included a more precise explanation of how people enter God's kingdom. Jesus had indicated this obscurely by telling Nicodemus, "Very truly, I tell you, no one can see the kingdom of God without being born from above" (John 3:3). This latter phrase is sometimes translated "born again." The author soon adds, "And just as Moses lifted up the serpent in the wilderness, so must the Son of Man be lifted up, that whosoever believes in him may have eternal life" (v. 14). "Son of Man" refers to Jesus. This lifting up envisions Jesus being lifted onto the cross to die for our sins. People who repent of their sins and believe in Jesus's atoning death for them will be divinely forgiven of their sins and inherit eternal life (vv. 16, 36).[8]

Yet, Jesus's mention of the mechanism of being born again was not new. It was foreshadowed in the Torah. Moses compared outward circumcision to inner repentance when he exhorted the people of Israel, "Circumcise, then, the foreskin of your heart" (Deuteronomy 10:16; cf. 30:6; Jeremiah 4:4). And the prophet Ezekiel says to Israel on behalf of God concerning the world to come, "I will cleanse you. A new heart I will give you, and a new spirit I will put within you" (Ezekiel 36:25–26).

So, the New Testament gospel is about the promised kingdom. But it must have a king, and that king is Jesus. He must first bear the sins of his people while hanging on the cross before he can sit on his throne of majesty to become their king. Therefore, *the cross must come before the crown.*

After Jesus's death, the Christian gospel includes his saving work on the cross. God proved this by raising him from the dead, which also vindicated him. By believing in Jesus Christ as our personal Savior from our sins and that God raised him from the dead, we are born anew by the Spirit of God and thereby spiritually enter his kingdom.

The website for the New International Version of the Bible is thenivbible.com. It has a one-page article entitled "What Does 'Gospel' Mean?" It answers, "The crucifixion and resurrection of Jesus stand at the center of the Christian gospel message. Thus, the gospel Paul

---

[8] Christians have held various viewpoints of Jesus's atonement.

preached was this: 'that Christ died for our sins according to the Scriptures, that he was buried, that he was raised on the third day according to the Scriptures, and that he appeared to Cephas [Peter], and then to the Twelve' (1 Corinthians 15.3–5)." We will examine this most important gospel text later, in the chapter about Paul.

These two faith requirements—the atoning death of the Lord Jesus Christ and his resurrection from the dead—are the two essentials of faith required to receive salvation. *All other Christian teaching lying outside of this gospel is unnecessary to believe for salvation.* That is why Paul calls it "the gospel of your salvation" and "the gift of God" (Ephesians 1:13; 2:8). The only way to receive it is by repentance and faith. Having been condemned by God as sinners, we are justified before him by faith (see John 3:16–18).

An example of what is *not* an essential requirement to believe for salvation is Jesus's virgin birth even though Christians often have thought it is. Two narratives of it are in Matthew 1:18–25 and Luke 1:26–35. But Jesus's virgin birth is never mentioned again in the New Testament, thus not in any faith requirements regarding the gospel.

The Christian gospel, therefore, answers two questions: (1) Who was Jesus and (2) What did he do? The answer to the first question is that Jesus was God's "anointed one," which means Messiah (Heb. *mashiach*). The answer to the second question is God sent Jesus to die as our Savior from condemnation for our sins. God then raised Jesus from the dead to become "Lord" of all the earth. That is why Christians proclaim "the Lord Jesus Christ." So the notion that Jesus is God incarnate *is not* part of the Christian gospel that must be believed for salvation. Church fathers *added* it to the gospel without divine authorization, which we will examine later.

Billy Graham's Sermon: "The ABCs of The Gospel"

In 1949, when I was seven years old, my mother attended a Billy Graham Crusade in Seattle, and she took me with her. Billy preached the gospel—the good news about Jesus Christ—and it caused her to cry. I had never seen her cry like that. I then thought that when I grow up, I want to know what that man said that made my mother cry.

In time, I wanted to meet Billy Graham. And I did, in about 1970. It was because Billy loved to play golf. I met him on the putting green at the Atlanta Country Club as we were preparing to play the pro-am during the PGA Tour's Atlanta Classic. That is when I learned that Billy Graham didn't always get everything right. *He called me Zermit three times*! I had been called Kermit the Hermit many times; but not *Zermit*.

Billy Graham spoke to our PGA Tour Bible Study three different times. But before that, one year our group hosted a dinner for all Tour pros playing in the Atlanta Classic to hear Billy Graham speak. A majority of the 150 pros in the tournament attended. I sat next to Jack Nicklaus, since I had invited him. Billy Graham titled his sermon "The ABCs of the Gospel." In delivering this message, Billy explained that the letter *A* stood for "acknowledge your sin," which is repentance; *B* stood for "believe Jesus Christ died for your sins and rose from the dead;" and *C* stood for "confess Jesus as Lord." Folks, that is the gospel of the New Testament, plain and simple! No "Jesus is God" in it.

Church Fathers Corrupted the Gospel

So, *church fathers corrupted the gospel by adding to it that Jesus is God* and requiring people to believe this to be forgiven of their sins, be saved, and thus become a genuine Christian. What exactly do I mean that church fathers *corrupted* the gospel?

The verb *corrupt* means to ruin or reduce the character, quality, or integrity of someone or something. "To corrupt" is often used to refer to illegal or immoral behavior. But "to corrupt" also can mean to contaminate with error. And that is how I am using it by alleging that *church fathers corrupted the gospel*. I do not mean they *destroyed* the gospel, making it worthless. I mean they *contaminated the gospel with error*.

The result was that they made the Christian gospel somewhat *different* from what it was originally. That is, they infected or tainted the pure gospel, making it "spoiled" as the Latin word *corruptus* means. They even made it more *difficult* to become a Christian because many people rejected Christianity since it seemed nonsensical to them that God would, or even could, become a man. Because of this, I will call this alteration by church fathers "the patristic gospel" in contradistinction to "the primitive gospel" of the Bible's New Testament.

Nevertheless, when people believe this corrupted, patristic gospel, they still believe its proclamation that Jesus Christ died for their sins and rose from the dead as Savior and Lord, which brings them salvation. However, *the patristic addition that Jesus is God has nothing to do with the original gospel*. Christians need to excise this corruption and thereby return to the unadulterated purity of the primitive gospel.

The primitive gospel of the earliest Christians was minimalist compared to the patristic gospel of later church fathers. I noticed this difference in the New Testament when I was a Trinitarian, during my twenties and thirties, thus prior to my becoming a non-Trinitarian. I had many long discussions about theology with friends and others who were Mormons and Jehovah Witnesses. I often concluded they likely were genuine Christians because they met the minimalist faith requirements of the New Testament gospel even though they often did not adhere exactly to the doctrine of the Trinity. My decision about them was contrary to that of my evangelical church community, which ironically has always been "the Bible church movement."

I believe that many Christians are too focused on their own church community and thereby become too myopic theologically. In time, the Catholic Church became increasingly maximalist both theologically and ecclesiastically. This resulted in rivalry between differing religious communities that were professedly Christian. Oftentimes, these differences were theological even though the New Testament said little or nothing about the issues disputed. Moreover, the Catholic Church adopted a narrow, schismatic, and arrogant attitude by saying "there is no salvation outside the Catholic Church." That is why the Protestant Reformation had to happen, which I believe generally was of God.

Intense rivalry between genuine church communities is sin. Wise King Solomon wrote something three thousand years ago that surely applies to this situation. He said, "I saw that all toil and all skill in work come from one person's envy of another. This also is vanity and a chasing after wind" (Ecclesiastes 4:4). Embracing the minimalist, original gospel of the early Christians reduces such rivalry, encourages ecumenism, and thus better achieves "the unity of the Spirit in the bond of peace" (Ephesians 4:3).

Paul Warned about "Another Jesus" and "a Different Gospel"

About one-fourth of the New Testament consists of the apostle Paul's letters. Many distinguished scholars now agree that they do not contain any clear identification that Jesus is God. Traditionalists often cite three Pauline texts as doing so: Romans 9:5; Titus 2:13; and 2 Thessalonians 1:12. But all three have grammatical problems in which they can be understood to say Jesus is God or not say this. Yet in Paul's several texts in which he defines his gospel, such as Romans 10:9–10 and 1 Corinthians 15:1–4, he does not say Jesus is God. So the gospel that Paul preached did not identify Jesus as God.

Paul sometimes encountered people who preached a message about Jesus that differed seriously from his own. He warned the Corinthian believers, "I am afraid that, as the serpent deceived Eve by his cunning, your thoughts will be led astray from a sincere and pure devotion to Christ. For if someone comes and proclaims another Jesus than the one we proclaimed, or if you receive a different spirit from the one you received, or a different gospel from the one you accepted, you put up with it readily enough" (2 Corinthians 11:3–4).

Paul wrote similarly to the churches of Galatia, in Galatians 1:6–9):

> I am astonished that you are so quickly deserting the one who called you in the grace of Christ and are turning to a different gospel—not that there is another gospel, but there are some who are confusing you and want to pervert the gospel of Christ. But even if we or an angel from heaven should proclaim to you a gospel contrary to what we proclaimed to you, let that one be accursed! As we have said before, so now I repeat, if anyone proclaims to you a gospel contrary to what you have received, let that one be accursed!

Paul repeating this bold denunciation indicates its importance.

So, is the original gospel that church fathers corrupted "another gospel"? And is the Jesus they proclaimed, whom they said is a God-man, "another Jesus"? I don't think the apostle Paul would have gone that far in condemning their error. Why? The patristic gospel contains the saving message of faith in Jesus's atoning death and resurrection. Paul surely referred to some false teachers who were guilty of teaching much worse error. They likely did not believe in Jesus's atoning death and resurrection at all.

Besides Paul, the New Testament's letter of Jude is full of dire warnings. One of them seems to be about changing the gospel. For Jude writes, "Beloved, while eagerly preparing to write to you about the salvation we share, I find it necessary to write and appeal to you to contend for the faith that was once for all entrusted to the saints. For certain intruders have stolen in among you" to teach false doctrine (Jude 3–4). So, like Paul, Jude seems to warn against people changing the primitive Christian gospel.

The Simplicity of the Christian Gospel

In the text above, 2 Corinthians 11:3–4, wherein Paul warns of false teachers who preach "another Jesus" and thus a "different gospel," the NRSVue and other versions have Paul explaining that this error will lead people "astray from a sincere and pure devotion to Christ." The KJV translates it "the simplicity that is in Christ" (cf. NASB).

Simplicity is the hallmark of the primitive gospel. In contrast, complexity and incomprehension are more prone to error regarding God's truth. Accordingly, it is much simpler to comprehend that Jesus was no more than a man than him being a God-man who has two natures, divine and human, and that he is "the Second Person of the Trinity," all which cannot be found in the Bible.

When Christians disagree about their religion, they should appeal to the Bible as the final arbiter of faith and practice. Paul wrote, "All scripture is inspired by God and is useful for teaching, for reproof, for correction, and for training in righteousness, so that the person may be proficient, equipped for every good work" (2 Timothy 3:16).

Further evidence that the doctrine of the Trinity is not supported in the Bible is that Trinitarians often must argue that their doctrine, "three is one," is a mystery that is incomprehensible to humans. *That is nonsense!* According to that, Trinitarians don't understand it either! So why should we listen to them? Moreover, this *non sequitur* argument about mystery could be applied to just about any false proposition.

Because church fathers changed the gospel of the New Testament, Jewish Bible scholar Joseph Klausner rightly stated, "The Messiahship of Jesus became secondary to his deity."[9]

To end this chapter, I will quote from *The Restitution* (p. 67):

The Nicene-Chalcedonian Christology of the institutional Catholic Church represents a departure from the true gospel handed down by the apostles of Jesus Christ, and this departure was "expansionist." We can err by ascribing too much to Jesus Christ just as we can err by ascribing too little to Him. When Christians ascribe too much to Jesus, they inevitably ascribe too little to God the Father. Therefore, when traditionalists have been expansionist in their Christology, it automatically made them reductionist in their theology proper.

---

[9] Joseph Klausner, *The Messianic Idea in Israel: From Its Beginning to the Completion of the Mishnah*, tr. W. F. Stinespring (New York: MacMillan, 1955), 528.

Chapter 3
The Gospel According to Church Fathers

Categorizing Church Fathers

Christianity has often had to wrestle theologically with pagan opposition outside the church and internal division inside the church. Mostly due to the latter, the Catholic Church held seven so-called "ecumenical councils" between 325 CE and 787 CE to settle some theological disputes. Those who were influential in these councils were bishops and some priests deemed as "church fathers." The church cited the apostolic council of the early church, reported in Acts 15, as precedent for these ecumenical councils.

"Church fathers" refers preeminently to theologians during the patristic era known for their writings. "Apostolic fathers" were those who lived in the late first and early second centuries and knew one or more of Jesus's twelve apostles or were much influenced by someone who knew them. "Post-apostolic fathers" guided church doctrine during the patristic era, which existed from the late second century through the eighth century. They are categorized in relation to the Nicene Council of 325. Thus, "ante-Nicene fathers" lived in the second and third centuries prior to 325. "Nicene church fathers" lived in most of the fourth century. "Post-Nicene church fathers" lived from the late fourth century through the eighth century.

Ante-Nicene Church Fathers

Many ante-Nicene fathers were called "apologists" since they defended Christian faith against the pagan world, largely through their writings. They should be respected for doing this and teaching the core elements of the Christian gospel. Those are that the one God created the universe, sent Jesus of Nazareth to die on the cross for our sins, and raised him from the dead. These ante-Nicene fathers also taught that Jesus was God, yet essentially subordinate to the Father. They deemed Jesus as having a lesser divinity than that of the Father. They regarded only the Father as "the Almighty" and "the one God."

Although most ante-Nicene fathers identified Jesus as "God" in their writings, they never made this proclamation an essential of the gospel. Ignatius (c. 40–110/117 CE), Bishop of Antioch, emerges as the first patristic writer to unequivocally call Jesus "God." Yet, in the several letters wherein he does so, he never designates it as part of the gospel, meaning that which must be believed to receive salvation. Likewise, leading apologists Justin Martyr, Irenaeus, Clement of Alexandria, Tertullian, Hippolytus, and Origen identify Jesus as "God" in their writings without saying this proposition must be believed to be a Christian. But this situation changed most dramatically in 325.

The Nicene Council

The first ecumenical church council was in 325. Called "the Council of Nicaea," it was the first and most august body of all seven church councils. Its creed became the most significant turning point in the history of the development of church Christology.

These councils were named according to the places where they were held. Nicaea was in present Iznik, Turkey. In 313, the new Roman Emperor Constantine (c. 272–337) had become a professing Christian (without baptism) and made Christianity the primary religion in his empire. Yet he did not force his citizens to be Christians. In 325, he summoned the Nicene Council to settle a theological dispute that had erupted in the church that was disrupting the peace of his empire. I relate in *The Restitution* (p. 44):

> The Council of Nicaea remains to this day the most important event in the history of post-apostolic Christianity. The Catholic Church has always described it as "the first ecumenical council" and "the great and holy council" because it was to become the first and most illustrious of all subsequent ecumenical church councils. ... Bishops were summoned from throughout the empire, and 318 reportedly attended ... each bishop was accompanied by two presbyters and three servants, so that perhaps 2,000 men attended. All were guests of the emperor at his expense, and the affair lasted just over two months during mid-year.

What was the dispute about? In the second and third centuries, the apologists taught that Jesus preexisted as the Logos. They had borrowed from Greek philosophy a well-known concept that the creator of the universe related to his creation by means of a pantheon of aeons, of which the Logos was supreme. The apologists used this Logos concept, mentioned in the Gospel of John, to teach that Jesus preexisted as "the Logos-Son," with the latter referring to him as "the Son of God." They deemed this Logos-Son as "a lesser God" who was essentially subordinate to God the Father. R. P. C. Hanson says this dispute "was the problem of how to reconcile two factors which were part of the very fabric of Christianity: monotheism and the worship of Jesus as divine."[10]

Origen (185–254) of Alexandria, Egypt, was the first patristic theologian who wrote a systematic theology. He was much influenced by Greek philosophy in doing so. That is why he taught the preexistence and salvation (universalism) of all human souls. He differed from the apologists by claiming the Logos-Son existed eternally yet was begotten. This "eternal generation," as it was called, is an oxymoron that aided the later Trinitarians in claiming their doctrine is a "mystery" that humans cannot comprehend.

Also at Alexandria, Egypt—the third largest diocese in the Roman Empire—an elderly man named Arius (c. 250–336), a church presbyter (deacon), taught the Logos-Son was *not* eternal and *was* subordinate to God. For support, he cited church father Tertullian, who said of the Logos-Son, "There was a time when he was not." This meant God had created the Logos-Son prior to the creation of the universe. This led Arius to also claim that the Logos-Son was "like" God the Father, but not of "the same essence."

Thus, Arius taught against Origen's eternal generation. This dispute signaled that the Church was headed down a rabbit hole of intellectual futility from which would arise a creed of massive influence to this day. I relate in *The Restitution* (pp. 43, 46–47):

> Bishop Alexander objected vehemently. He was one of the most powerful bishops in the Roman Empire, with his jurisdiction encompassing much of North Africa. Bishop Alexander denounced Arius's teaching as heretical. He alleged that it rendered Christ as less than fully God and thus not God at all. He explained that God the Father generated the Logos-Son as a distinct personality but that, in order for Him to be fully God, there could never have been a time when the Logos-Son did not exist. The bishop opposed the apologists' teaching on this and affirmed Origen's contradictory doctrine of eternal generation. The bishop asserts, "God is always, the Son is always," and the Son is "the unbegotten

---

[10] R. P. C. Hanson, *The Search for the Christian Doctrine of God: The Arian Controversy, 318–381* (orig. 1988; Grand Rapids: Baker Academic, 2005), xx.

begotten." ... Debate ensued primarily because the word *homoousios* was introduced into the creed. By applying it to Jesus, it rendered Him as being of the "same substance" (Gr. *homo*=same; *ousia*=substance) with the Father. ... Thus, this disagreement at Nicaea centered mostly on the words *homoousios* and *homoiousios*, a difference of the letter "i."

Bishop Alexander started this controversy with a letter signed by 200 bishops. In it, he condemned Arius as "an unbelieving soul," not "a disciple of Christ." So, Emperor Constantine sent a letter to both men, delivered by his spiritual advisor Hosius, which said:

> Having made a careful enquiry into the origin and foundation of these differences, I find the cause to be a truly insignificant character, and quite unworthy of such fierce contention. ... For how very few are there able either accurately to comprehend, or adequately to explain, subjects so sublime and abstruse in their nature? ... For as long as you contend about these small and very insignificant questions, it is not fitting that so large a portion of God's people should be under the direction of your judgment, ... you who wrangle together on points so trivial and altogether unessential ... Let us withdraw ourselves with a good will from these temptations of the devil.[11]

Many Trinitarians have accused the emperor of ignorance. But the letter is quite biblical, and some historians have claimed Hosius wrote it. Much of this dispute consisted of a nuance of words. Edward Gibbon famously said of it in his critically acclaimed seven-volume history of the Roman Empire, "the profane of every age have derided the furious contests which the difference of a single diphthong excited between the Homoousians and the Homoiousians."[12]

The Nicene Creed

Catholic Church councils usually drafted dogmatic statements of belief called "creeds." They served as a test of orthodoxy, meaning "right opinion." Roman emperors often pressured bishops to draft such creeds, expecting they would settle disputes.

---

[11] Eusebius of Caesarea, *The Life of Constantine*, in *Nicene and Post-Nicene Fathers*: Series 2, Book II, Chapters LXIV-LXXI.
[12] Edward Gibbon, *The History of the Decline and Fall of the Roman Empire*, 7 vols. (London: Methuen, 1909), 2:373.

The Nicene Council drafted its Nicene Creed and made it official. Its most critical portion for us, translated from Greek, says Jesus is "very God from very God" or "truly God from truly God." It adds that Jesus is "of one substance with the Father," so that they are exactly alike. This creed concludes with a list of six sayings uttered by Arius and his followers that represent objections to these two precepts. The creed then declares of these Arians: "They are condemned by the catholic and apostolic Church."

So, Arius and his followers believed Jesus had a lesser deity than the Father did. They did not believe Jesus was "very God from very God," meaning just as much God as the Father is God. The council would have condemned even more folks who do not believe Jesus is God *at all*, such as me, no matter what we *do* believe about Jesus.

The New Testament does not have any express statement saying Jesus is God, especially in any of its material about the gospel. The book of Acts shows that this is *not* what the early disciples of Jesus were proclaiming in their evangelistic messages. (We will examine the book of Acts in Chapter 6.) Plus, this Nicene declaration that Jesus is God conflicts with the Apostles Creed, which preceded the Nicene Creed.

The Apostles Creed most rightly begins, "I believe in God the Father almighty; and in Christ Jesus His only Son, our Lord." Then it says no more about Jesus's identity. So, the Apostles Creed does not say Jesus is God, let alone make such a precept a necessary faith condition for receiving God's salvation as the later Nicene Creed does.

The Nicene Creed begins, "We believe in one God, the Father almighty." This is the same as in the Apostles Creed except the word "one" is added. It strangely suggests only the Father is God; yet this creed later says Jesus is "very God from very God." Since this means Jesus is just as much God as the Father, these two seem contradictory.

Athanasius: "The Great Defender" of the Nicene Creed

The Nicene Council consisted of three factions in this dispute. Bishop Alexander led the so-called "orthodox party." His secretary was twenty-seven-year-old Athanasius. Three years later Alexander died, and Athanasius succeeded him as bishop. Athanasius became known as "the great defender" of the deity of Christ and thus the Nicene Creed for decades afterward even though the creed was not fully accepted. Several emperors during this period were Arian in belief. Thus, I write in *The Restitution* (p. 55),

> Trinitarian R.P.C. Hanson has authored the standard resource on the development of church Christology during the Arian

Controversy, a rubric he says is a misnomer.[13] He claims that (1) Hilary, Bishop of Potiers, started the idealization of Athanasius even though he never met him; (2) "The historians of the nineteenth century were even more laudatory" of him; (3) "The twentieth century, however, has in many instances altered the favourable verdict."[14] Hanson reveals that Athanasius's theological opponents accused him of committing undeserved beatings, woundings, imprisonments, and even murders, so that all Eastern bishops, who were mostly Arian, refused to communicate with him for at least twenty years.[15]

Athanasius's retort to these allegations is typical of cultists. He disassociates life and theology, as if they are unrelated. ... Hanson relates, "No one ever seriously accused Athanasius of heresy, but his writings suggest time and time again that accusations of misconduct as a bishop should be ignored in order to concentrate upon the doctrinal issues."[16] In contrast, Jesus taught that true knowledge of God and His Son can only be obtained through humility and obeying God.

Athanasius had a checkered career. Arian emperors banished him from the Roman Empire five times, forcing him to suffer exile for twenty years. But each time an emperor who embraced Nicene orthodoxy ascended to the throne, he quickly recalled Athanasius from exile and reinstated him to his see.

Athanasius was fond of name-calling. He often labeled Arians as Ariomaniacs. Since Arius was forty years older than Athanasius, Athanasius violated Paul's instruction, "Do not speak harshly to an older man, but speak to him as to a father" (1 Timothy 5:1). Hanson cites various historians who describe Athanasius as "an obstinate fanatic," "a political power-broker," and "like a modern gangster."[17] It appears that Sir Isaac Newton, one of the smartest men who ever lived, would have agreed with this.

Many people regard Sir Isaac Newton (1643–1727) as the greatest scientist ever. He was a devout Christian who wrote more about theology than he did about physics and mathematics combined. But he never published his theological views since he would have been severely punished for them because of England's Anglican Church, which was Trinitarian. Newton wrote that this was a major reason he disliked Athanasius.

---

[13] Hanson, *The Search for the Christian Doctrine of God*, xvii.
[14] Hanson, *The Search for the Christian Doctrine of God*, 239–40.
[15] Hanson, *The Search for the Christian Doctrine of God*, 249–54.
[16] Hanson, *The Search for the Christian Doctrine of God*, 244.
[17] Hanson, *The Search for the Christian Doctrine of God*, 240.

Newton was neither Arian nor Deist, yet he often has been characterized as being one or the other. He chastised both Arius and Athanasius for introducing metaphysical concepts about Jesus that are not in the Bible. And Newton criticized the Deism concept of the "clockwork universe" by writing that "a being, however perfect, without dominion, cannot be said to be 'Lord God.'" Newton's anti-Trinitarian friend John Locke, whose writings highly influenced America's Thomas Jefferson, wrote of Isaac Newton's "great knowledge in the Scriptures, wherein I know few his equals."

Sir Isaac Newton believed exactly as I do about Jesus's identity. That is mostly why he is one of my heroes. Newton wrote his own theological creed as a single paragraph. At the end of it he quotes 1 Corinthians 8.5–6, which says only the Father is God. He then concludes by saying Christians have "one God and one Lord in our worship." Sir Isaac also read diligently the patristic views about Jesus's identity. He became so incensed with the misconduct of Athanasius that he wrote a devastating book against him entitled *Paradoxical Questions concerning the morals & actions of Athanasius & his followers*.

Regarding Athanasius's books, he is most known for *Incarnation of the Word*. In it he adopts *theosis*, saying, "The Son of God was made man that we might be made god" (54:3).[18] Athanasius will become a god? Jesus said in his Sermon on the Mount, "Beware of false prophets, who come to you in sheep's clothing but inwardly are ravenous wolves. You will know them by their fruits" (Matthew 7:15–16). I'm not saying Athanasius was not a Christian. But his critics make you wonder when thinking of this saying of Jesus.

The Council of Constantinople and Its Creed

As the fourth century transpired, there was no official church doctrine of the Trinity. It is still widely written that the Nicene Creed contains the doctrine of the Trinity. Only people who have never read it can say that. It only says of the Holy Spirit, "I believe ... in the Holy Spirit." Eminent church historian Philip Schaff relates, "the Holy Spirit ... until the middle of the fourth century was never a subject of special controversy."[19]

---

[18] The Eastern Orthodox Church cites 2 Peter 1:4 and teaches *theosis*, which means at the resurrection the righteous will be deified or divinized, but not to the extent God is.
[19] Philip Schaff, *History of the Christian Church*, 3rd ed., 8 vols. (orig. 1858; rep. Grand

In the 370s, the three Cappadocians laid the groundwork for the next council. They were Basil the Great (330–379), bishop of Caesarea; his younger brother Gregory (c. 332–395), bishop of Nyssa; and their friend Gregory of Nazianzus (329–389), who later became Patriarch of Constantinople. All wrote treatises on an agreed formula, that God is three substances (Gr. *hypostases*) in one essence (Gr. *homoousia*). Critics alleged this was tritheism. So Basil wrote a book entitled *Against Those Who Falsely Accuse Us of Saying That There Are Three Gods*. Jews, and subsequently Muslims, have alleged ever since that Christians are polytheists due to their doctrine of the Trinity.

The second ecumenical council, the Council of Constantinople, was summoned in 381 by Roman Emperor Theodosius. Its purpose was to oppose Arianism by making the doctrine of the Trinity official. This was done by adopting the Nicene Creed but altering it to say the Holy Spirit is equally God. Yet this Nicene-Constantinopolitan Creed, as it came to be called, does not include the word "trinity" and omits the six condemnations of the Arians in the Nicene Creed. This second creed is what church congregations have recited ever since, usually without knowing these details. Thus, churchgoers often have identified the Nicene-Constantinopolitan Creed incorrectly as the Nicene Creed.

It is questionable that these two councils should have been called "ecumenical." Both were held in the eastern branch of the Roman Empire and conducted in the Greek language. All bishops who attended them—318 at Nicaea and 150 at Constantinople—spoke Greek as their native language. Yet the capital of the Roman Empire was Rome, where Latin was the dominant language. The second council was later relabeled the First Council of Constantinople since another council was held there in 553 that had to be called the Second Council of Constantinople. All bishops who attended in 381 were from the east except six that were from western North Africa. Thus, all these so-called "ecumenical councils" were dominated by the eastern branch of the Catholic Church. Ecumenical means a complete representation of churches, indicating their unity.

The Council of Chalcedon and Its Definition

The Council of Chalcedon was held in 451 CE to establish officially how Jesus is both man and God. Its "Definition of Faith" sort of serves as a creed. It cites and affirms the creeds of Nicaea and Constantinople and declares the Virgin Mary is *Theotokos*, meaning "God-bearer" or

---

Rapids: Eerdmans, 1985), 2:560.

"mother of God." This Definition of Faith is known mostly for saying, "our Lord Jesus Christ is ... perfect in Godhead, the Same perfect in manhood, truly God and truly man. ... known in two natures, without confusion, without change, without division, without separation." This designation of Jesus having two natures came to be called "the hypostatic union of Christ."

This Chalcedonian Definition of Faith has one sentence containing more than two hundred words that explains in detail about Jesus having two natures. It concludes, "The prophets have taught concerning Him, and as the Lord Jesus Christ Himself hath taught us." *That is a bald-faced lie*! There is nothing in the Bible about Jesus having two natures or that he taught this about himself. For this, the Chalcedonian Definition ought not be trusted.

This Chalcedonian Definition of Faith twice targets those "daring to corrupt the mystery of the (Lord's) incarnation" and "denying the title 'Theotokos' to the virgin." The later Protestant Reformation rejected that Mary is *Theotokos*. But early Protestant leaders did not go far enough in scrutinizing these creeds regarding their assertions that Jesus is God, he has two natures, and God is three Persons.

This Chalcedonian Definition of Faith is lengthy. In its English translation it has 1,619 words, whereas the Apostles Creed has only 83 words. Wise King Solomon wrote, "let your words be few. ... The more words, the more vanity" (Ecclesiastes 5:2; 6:11). Indeed, this Definition repeatedly praises the council as "the holy, great, and ecumenical synod." Four times it says the Nicene Council was attended by 318 "church fathers" who were bishops, and three times it says the Council of Constantinople had 150 bishops. This seems to have been done as if having large numbers of bishops signify the creeds must be correct. What they don't say is these councils were controlled by politics.

Could Church Councils Have Been Wrong?

Some Christians have told me the ecumenical church councils could not have been wrong in deciding Jesus is God. They claim the Holy Spirit would have prevented church fathers from making such a grievous error. Dr. S. Lewis Johnson told me that. He wrote the foreword in my first book, *The Gospels Interwoven*, endorsed by Billy Graham. But, then, Johnson was a 5-point Calvinist, which sort of explains his assertion.

In human history, large numbers of people have been wrong about many things. For instance, the Roman Catholic Church banned books by Catholic scientists Galileo and Copernicus that correctly taught that our solar system is heliocentric. The Church was following conventional wisdom by claiming an Earth-centric solar system. So, it charged Galileo with "heresy" and house-arrested him for the remainder of his life.

Church historian Philip Jenkins says the ecumenical councils erred. (*Forbes* magazine says of him, "Jenkins is one of America's top religious scholars.") He says they were not always that spiritual and often were controlled by politics. He lays it all out in his highly acclaimed book with a shocking title that tells it all—*The Jesus Wars: How Four Patriarchs, Three Queens, and Two Emperors Decided What Christians Would Believe for the Next 1,500 Years*. It documents the first six ecumenical councils with special focus on the two-natures debate at the Council of Chalcedon. Jenkins says, "Through all the christological debates, the empire acted as a force within the church ... The government was absolutely involved in church debates at all stages." He further alleges most alarmingly, "The councils led to outrageous violence in many parts of the empire—to popular uprisings and coups 'd'état, to massacres and persecutions."[20]

Patristic Logos Speculation Led to Increasing Error

The Bible warns about venturing beyond its divine revelation into speculative theorizing in what may be called "theologizing." For instance, Moses explains, "The secret things belong to the LORD our God, but the revealed things belong to us and to our children forever" (Deuteronomy 29:29). Likewise, King David says in his song lyrics in the psalter, "LORD, my heart is not lifted up; my eyes are not raised too high; I do not occupy myself with things too great and too marvelous for me" (Psalm 131:1).

Post-apostolic church fathers engaged in "logos speculation" by misusing a text in the Gospel of John as their starting point. It states, "the Word became flesh," referring to Jesus (John 1:14). The logos concept was prevalent in the Hellenistic world wherein church fathers lived. I tell about this in *The Restitution* (pp. xvi–xvii) as follows:

> But this speculative mode of thinking is what led church fathers into their christological morass. They sought detailed answers to theological

---

[20] Philip Jenkins, *The Jesus Wars: How Four Patriarchs, Three Queens, and Two Emperors Decided What Christians Would Believe for the Next 1,500 Years* (New York: HarperCollins, 2010), 103, 25.

questions about the nature of the Logos and its relation to Jesus, Jesus's supposed preexistence and its time of origin, and thus the exact and full extent of Jesus's uniqueness. ... Church fathers amplified these mistakes by stating their dogmatic speculations sometimes in non-scriptural, metaphysical language and categories borrowed from Greek religio-philosophy. Since error tends to compound itself in time, in succeeding centuries the church fell into a labyrinth of heinous blunders of doctrinal complexity exacerbated by its ecumenical councils and creeds. Due to scriptural silence on these christological matters, these church fathers should have been more flexible by permitting some degree of intellectual freedom on these issues. *Until glory comes, the precise extent of Jesus's uniqueness must remain for us a mystery to contemplate rather than a problem to solve.*

So, Nicene church fathers *added* to the gospel of the New Testament their logos speculation. They set it forth in their Nicene Creed by declaring that Jesus is "very God from very God." They did this to indicate their belief that Jesus preexisted eternally and thus was God just as much as the Father is God. And they made this axiom a necessary element of the gospel that must be believed to receive God's salvation. By adding these declarations, to some extent these Nicene church fathers *corrupted* the Christian gospel.

Because of this, Nicene church fathers violated two Old Testament texts. Moses warned not to add to the Torah, and this injunction justly applies to these Christians about the gospel. Moses said to Israel, "You must neither add anything to what I command you nor take away anything from it" (Deuteronomy 4:2). The following biblical proverb certainly applies as well, "Every word of God proves true ... Do not add to his words, or else he will rebuke you, and you will be found a liar" (Proverbs 30:5–6).

Chapter 4
The Gospel According to Matthew, Mark, and Luke

Scholars call the first three gospels of the New Testament—Matthew, Mark, and Luke—"the Synoptics." And they label their supposed authors "the Synoptists." This is because each book is a synopsis of Jesus's public ministry, death, and resurrection. This brief period in his life likely lasted only two or three years. These three gospels are similar, frequently reporting the same events in Jesus's ministry and his same sayings. Yet the reporting has significant differences that scholars call "the Synoptic problem." We will not examine this subject since it is a complex study that does not concern our topic. Instead, this chapter is about whether these three gospels identify Jesus as "God."

The Gospel of the Kingdom

These three gospels tell the good news that Jesus proclaimed about the kingdom of God and sometimes his relationship to it. Matthew relates that John the Baptist and Jesus preached the same message, "Repent, for the kingdom of heaven has come near" (Matthew 3:2; 4:17). So they made national penitence a prerequisite for Israel to be given the kingdom that had been promised in the Jewish Scriptures (Old Testament). Also, Jesus often taught parables about this kingdom—what it is like and how to enter it.

Mark begins his gospel similarly with this introduction, "The beginning of the good news of Jesus Christ" (Mark 1:1).[21] Mark identifies who Jesus is, saying he is the Christ, but not saying he is God. Mark further recounts, "Jesus came to Galilee proclaiming the good news of God and saying, 'The time is fulfilled, and the kingdom of God has come near; repent, and believe in the good news'" (Mark 1:14–15). People who say "No regrets" don't seem to believe in repentance. But fearing God and repenting of sins are prerequisites for attaining wisdom and experiencing God by entering his kingdom.

---

[21] Some Greek manuscripts add *huiou theou* ("Son of God").

So, according to this message, God's program for his chosen nation Israel is that he has predetermined that if Israel repents, he will give it the promised kingdom. John the Baptist therefore was calling people to repent and be baptized in the Jordan River as an outward symbol of that inner penitence, which results in cleansing of the soul.

In modern times, scholars have arrived at a consensus that the kingdom Jesus preached was both "already" and "not yet." "Already" means God's kingdom is here now in a spiritual sense. That is, it is in the hearts of God's people and thus cannot be visibly seen. "Not yet" indicates God's kingdom is eschatological, meaning it is not here in all its glory, but it will appear when Jesus returns at his "second coming" (Hebrews 9:27).

Luke says Jesus revealed another aspect of God's kingdom when he said, "The kingdom of God is among you" (Luke 17:21). Jesus likely meant he was the embodiment of the kingdom (cf. 11:20). When he preached this kingdom, Jesus sometimes referred to himself since he was the way into it (John 14:6). That is what he meant when he said, "I am the gate" (10:7).

Yet, for Jesus, the cross had to come before the crown. All three Synoptists report that on three occasions Jesus clearly told his apostles in private that the religious authorities at Jerusalem would get him killed, and he would arise from the dead on the third day (Matthew 16:31; 17:23; 20:18–19 and parallels). Luke informs that after all of this occurred, the risen Jesus appeared to his gathered disciples and said to them, "Was it not necessary that the Messiah should suffer these things and then enter into his glory?" (Luke 24:26). He later added, "Thus it was written, that the Messiah is to suffer and to rise from the dead on the third day; and that repentance and forgiveness of sins is to be proclaimed in his name to all nations, beginning at Jerusalem" (vv. 46–47). The good news about the kingdom of God, therefore, included Jesus's atoning death and resurrection.

Jesus Is the Messiah But Not God

In Chapter 1, I related that I began my research into whether Jesus is God by reading only what he said of himself as reported in the New Testament gospels. And I discovered there is nothing in them in which he expressly stated, or even hinted, that he was God or a God-man. Here is what I wrote about this subject in *The Restitution* (p. 8):

> The importance of the self-consciousness of Jesus for Christology cannot be overemphasized. If a person accepts the premise that both

the pre- and post-Easter Jesus of the NT became the source and center of early Christianity, as this author does, *Jesus's self-consciousness is the preeminent issue to investigate in an attempt to determine His identity.* The institutional church and radical critics have surprisingly undervalued this aspect. In fact, they have opposed it, albeit for opposite reasons. *Any fundamental belief in Jesus's identity that cannot be connected to Jesus's self-consciousness, as gleaned from the NT gospels, is seriously flawed and represents a discontinuity in one's Christology.*

I then decided that the next most important part of my research into this subject of whether Jesus is God should be what Jesus's apostles said about his identity. So that took me back to the time when Jesus chose his apostles.

Early in Jesus's public ministry, when he began to choose his twelve apostles, they believed what Philip told Nathanael, "We have found him about whom Moses in the Law and also the Prophets wrote, Jesus son of Joseph from Nazareth" (John 1:45). When Philip then brought Nathanael to meet Jesus, he spoke supernaturally to him like a prophet by saying, "'I saw you under the fig tree before Philip called you.' Nathanael replied, 'Rabbi, you are the Son of God! You are the King of Israel!'" (v. 49).

All three Synoptists report that Jesus later asked his apostles who they thought he was.[22] They didn't say he was God. That never entered their minds. Why? Jesus never said it of himself. If he had, it would have seemed pagan because other ancient religions were polytheistic by teaching myths about some gods becoming both god and human. In contrast, Jews were monotheistic, believing only in one God who is the Creator of the universe. In fact, their Bible states most succinctly, "God is not a man" (Numbers 23:19).

We read of Jesus's inquiry, "Now when Jesus came into the district of Caesarea Philippi, he asked his disciples, 'Who do people say that the Son of Man is?'" referring to himself (Matthew 16:13). They gave various answers and he continued, "'But who do you say that I am?' Simon Peter answered, 'You are the Messiah, the Son of the living God.' And Jesus answered him, 'Blessed are you, Simon son of Jonah! For flesh and blood has not revealed this to you but my Father in heaven'" (vv. 15–17). Jesus's reply indicates he approved of Peter's answer. Yet

---

[22] Matthew 16:13–16; Mark 8:27–29; Luke 9:18–20.

Peter did not say Jesus was God. It is far greater to be God than it is to be the human Messiah of Israel.

Knowing the Identity of God and Jesus

One of my favorite New Testament scholars is Roman Catholic Raymond E. Brown. I have seven of his books, mostly large ones, in my library. Early in his career, Brown, who is Trinitarian, wrote a small book the size of this one entitled *Jesus God and Man*. In it, he examines whether the major, critical New Testament texts identify Jesus as "God." He decides that only three clearly do—John 1:1c, 20:28, and Hebrews 1:8. He observes, "The use of 'God' for Jesus is rare in the New Testament." Then he adds, "In the Gospels Jesus never uses the title 'God' of himself." Even though Brown and I disagree about whether the Bible says Jesus is God, he rightly warns:

> Christian believers whose spiritual lives should be shaped by the Master, if they have not wrestled in some mature way with the identity of Jesus, are in danger of constructing a fictional Jesus. ... Most people answer the question of the identity of Jesus without any real struggle to gain precision about what the NT says. ... Christology is so important an issue for religious adherence that one should not express judgments without seriously looking at the evidence.[23]

It can be difficult for Trinitarian Christians to consider objectively if the Bible really does teach that Jesus is God. It requires critical thinking. That doesn't come easy for most of us who have had our minds made up about this subject for many years, as I did. But that is what a Bible student should strive to do, to think objectively and have an inquiring mind. Jesus said much about this regarding our effort to learn God's truth.

In the Sermon on the Mount, Jesus cautioned people not to be so hypercritical (Matthew 7:1–5). Then he said, "Ask, and it will be given to you; search, and you will find; knock, and the door will be opened for you. For everyone who asks receives, and everyone who searches finds, and for everyone who knocks, the door will be opened" (vv. 7–8). I said in Chapter 1 that this saying of Jesus is the main reason that the most frequent prayer of my life has been asking God to teach me his truth.

---

[23] Raymond E. Brown, *An Introduction to New Testament Christology* (New York: Paulist, 1994), 23, 86, vi, 10–11.

The Synoptic Jesus made an important statement about the necessity of having an inquiring mind and a humble attitude in seeking to know him and God the Father. Matthew (11:25–27) and Luke (10:21–22) record it nearly verbatim as a prayer. Matthew relates that Jesus said, "I thank you, Father, Lord of heaven and earth, because you have hidden these things from the wise and the intelligent and have revealed them to infants; yes, Father, for such was your gracious will. All things have been handed over to me by my Father; and no one knows the Son except the Father, and no one knows the Father except the Son and anyone to whom the Son chooses to reveal him."

The Gospel in Baptism and the Eucharist

The good news about Jesus's atoning death and resurrection is portrayed in the church's two rituals—baptism and Eucharist. Neither indicate Jesus is God.

All four gospels inform that John the Baptist immersed recipients in water as a symbol of their remission of sins. But this baptism later took on added meaning with church. The apostle Paul explains, "All of us who were baptized into Christ Jesus were baptized into his death," and "just as Christ was raised from the dead by the glory of the Father, so we also might walk in newness of life" (Romans 6:3–4). Paul informs elsewhere, "When you were buried with him in baptism, you were also raised with him through faith in the power of God, who raised him from the dead" (Colossians 2:12).

Jesus instituted the other ritual, "the Eucharist." Also called "the communion service" or "the Lord's supper" (1 Corinthians 11:20), all three synoptists report it.[24] Matthew relates, "While they were eating, Jesus took a loaf of bread, and after blessing it he broke it, gave it to the disciples, and said, 'Take, eat; this is my body.' Then he took a cup, and after giving thanks he gave it to them, saying, 'Drink from it, all of you, for this is my blood of the covenant, which is poured out for many for the forgiveness of sins'" (Matthew 26:26–28).

Roman Catholics and Protestants disagree about how to understand the Eucharist. I agree with Protestants, that Jesus intended the elements of bread and wine as no more than symbols signifying his imminent death by crucifixion. That is, the bread symbolizes Jesus's body crucified for us, and the wine symbolizes his blood shed for us. Roman Catholics insist these elements are, mystically, the actual body

---

[24] Matthew 26:26–29; Mark 14:22–25; Luke 22:1–-20; cf. 1 Corinthians 11:23–26.

and blood of Jesus, which they call "transubstantiation." Yet both sides agree that this most celebrated Christian ritual portrays Jesus dying for our sins. It does not signify Jesus being God or him having preexisted and having had an incarnation, but simply Jesus dying for us. Roman Catholics certainly emphasize this with the crucifix.

Church fathers included the gospels of Matthew, Mark, and Luke in the New Testament because they were read the most in the churches. Why? They contained the Eucharist and Jesus's crucifixion. The Gospel of Thomas has neither. Even in deciding the New Testament canon, the early Christians regarded Jesus dying for our sins as central to the gospel.

Jesus Is the "Son of God" But Not "God the Son"

In modern times, a consensus has rightly existed among New Testament scholars that the Synoptic Gospels do not contain anything indicating Jesus is God. Yet these gospels can identify Jesus as "the Son" or "Son of God." Some church fathers claimed Jesus being the Son of God meant he was God, and Christians have believed this ever since. Many Trinitarians have applied to Jesus the expressions "God the Son," "Second Person of the Trinity, and "divine Sonship," all of which are not in the Bible.

Since the Bible applies the epithet "son(s) of God" to others, this indicates calling Jesus "(the) Son of God" does not mean he is God. Examples of other "son(s) of God" in the Bible are angels (e.g., Job 1—2), the nation of Israel (Exodus 4:22; Hosea 11:1), kings of Israel (2 Samuel 7:14; 1 Chronicles 17:13), and often people. As for the Synoptics, Luke says the angel Gabriel told the virgin Mary that Jesus "will be called the Son of the Most High" and "Son of God" (Luke 1:32, 35; cf. 8:28; 20:36); yet Luke later relates that Jesus called his disciples "sons of the Most High" (6:35 NIV; cf. Matthew 5:9, 45). Plus, the apostle Paul calls believers "sons of God" (Romans 8:14, 19; Galatians 3:26).

The title "Messiah" means "anointed one," referring to mission, whereas the title "Son of God" depicts filial relationship. A possible example of the latter occurred at Jesus's baptism. When he arose from the water, a voice sounded that represented God the Father. All three Synoptists report the utterance similarly.[25] Matthew records, "And a voice from heaven said, 'This is my Son, the Beloved, with whom I am well pleased'" (Matthew 3:17). In this case, Son seems to refer to relationship or virgin birth.

---

[25] Matthew 3:17; Mark 1:11; Luke 3:22.

Yet the angel Gabriel said Jesus will be a "Son of God" due to his virgin birth (Luke 1:35). This signifies that Jesus's supernatural origin as a human being is of God. There is no biblical evidence suggesting that Jesus being the Son of God indicates a metaphysical, ontological genesis comparable to a man having a son. That is what many church fathers supposed, and most Christians ever since have believed.

All three Synoptists report that right after Jesus's baptism, the Holy Spirit led him into the wilderness, where he was tempted by Satan, the devil.[26] Matthew records three temptations. In two of them, Satan tempted Jesus by prefacing his remark, "If you are the Son of God" (Matthew 4:3, 6). If Jesus had been God, Satan surely would have known it and addressed him as "God" rather than "the Son of God."

There is other synoptic evidence indicating Jesus being the Son of God does not mean he is God. One is several instances in which the titles "the Messiah/Christ" and "the Son of God" are used interchangeably and applied to Jesus, indicating that they are synonymous. One such instance involved Jesus as an exorcist. Luke reports, "Demons also came out of many, shouting, 'You are the Son of God!' But he rebuked them and would not allow them to speak, because they knew that he was the Messiah" (Luke 4:41).

We have considered one example, when Jesus asked his apostles his identity. Matthew relates Peter answered, "You are the Messiah, the Son of the living God'" (Matthew 16:16). But Mark and Luke only record that Peter answered, "the Messiah." Their omission of "the Son of God" suggests the titles Messiah and Son of God were being used interchangeably and thus synonymously. Plus, only Matthew says Jesus replied, "Blessed are you, Simon son of Jonah! For flesh and blood has not revealed this to you but my Father in heaven" (v. 17). With this response, Jesus accepted Peter's answer as correct, that Jesus is indeed Israel's promised Messiah and the Son of God.

This synonymous use of titles is even more apparent in the interrogation of Jesus before the Sanhedrin. Only Matthew and Mark provide a full account of it.[27] According to Matthew, Caiaphas the high priest demanded of Jesus, "Tell us if you are the Messiah, the Son of God" (Matthew 26:63). He obviously meant these titles synonymously. (This praxis goes back to Psalm 2:2 and v. 7.) Also, the accusations in John 5:18 and 10:33, that Jesus claimed to be God, were never lodged

---

[26] Matthew 4:1–11; Mark 1:12–13; Luke 4:1–13.
[27] Matthew 26:57–68; Mark 14:53–65.

against him before the Sanhedrin. If those rulers had thought Jesus claimed to be God, that would have been a far greater crime with which to charge him.

Did Jesus Have to Be God to Save Us or Forgive Us?

Some Trinitarians claim, "Jesus had to be God to save us." They reason arbitrarily that only God can die as an atonement for our sins. But this notion makes soteriology determine Christology, which is backwards. And, most important, it's not in the Bible. Plus, God cannot die since he is "immortal" (1 Timothy 1:17; 6:16). If Trinitarians claim it was only Jesus's humanity that died, and it happened by him laying aside his deity, then he was no longer God. Also, the author of Hebrews indicates that Jesus could not have been both God and man to save us since "he had to become like his brothers in every respect ... to make a sacrifice of atonement for the sins of the people" (Hebrews 2:17). If Jesus was a God-man, he would not be like other Jews. And if he preexisted, as Trinitarians claim, Jesus would not be like other Jews since they did not preexist.

Where did this erroneous notion—that Jesus had to be God to save us—come from? It may have been borrowed from Manichaeans in Persia (present Iran) who believed in the Gnostic Redeemer Myth. It was the idea of a being sent from heaven to earth to *appear* human, enlighten people, and return to heaven. This myth existed no earlier than the second century CE. Christians could have adopted this idea after that.

Similarly, Trinitarians claim Jesus had to be God because he had authority to forgive sins. For support, they cite the pericope about Jesus healing a paralytic after he said to him, "Son, your sins are forgiven" (Mark 2:5).[28] Scribes then reasoned, "Who can forgive sins but God alone?" (v. 7). Trinitarians claim these scribes were right, signifying Jesus is God. Not so fast! Jesus refuted their opinion, saying of himself, "the Son of Man has authority on earth to forgive sins" (v. 10). Then he proved it by healing the man.

This Trinitarian interpretation suggests an ignorance of Jesus's status as God's agent par excellence. Jesus later indicated this, saying of God and himself, "The Father has life in himself, so he has granted the Son also to have life in himself, and he has given him authority to execute judgment" (John 5:26–27). Why did God give Jesus this

---

[28] This account appears in Matthew 9:1–8; Mark 2:1–12; Luke 5:17–26.

authority? Jesus explained it was "because he is the Son of Man" (v. 27). He was given divine authority to judge human beings and thereby forgive them of sins not because he was God but because he was the Son of Man. This is indicated in Daniel's vision of the Son of Man in Daniel 7:13–14. This vision depicts a royal coronation ceremony that will occur in heaven at "the end of days" on earth. Jesus, as "one like a Son of Man," will approach God, "the Ancient One," to receive the promised kingdom. Thus, as king of the entire world in the eschaton, Jesus will have authority derived from God to forgive sins.

Rather than Jesus having to be God to save us, he had to be fully human, as the Son of Man, to save us. That's what the author of Hebrews implies in Hebrews 2:17.

Conclusion

So, the Synoptic Gospels reveal that Jesus never said he was God, no character depicted therein said he was God, and the Synoptists don't say he was God. They say he was the Messiah/Christ, the Son of God, the Lord, and Master of his disciples, but not God Almighty. Since these gospels were so popular in the churches of the early centuries of Christianity, it is surprising that church fathers as early as the second century were saying Jesus is a lesser God than the Father and in the fourth century equally God with the Father. But they don't derive this from the gospels of Matthew, Mark, and Luke. Only with the Gospel of John do church fathers try to twist and contort such a declaration therefrom, to which we now turn.

Chapter 5
The Gospel According to John

Most New Testament documents contain the word *gospel* (Gr. *euangelion*) or its meaning—"good news." Yet the Gospel of John does not. Does this absence make this book less evangelistic? No. Many Christians have thought the Gospel of John is the most evangelistic document in the Bible. It is full of information about believing Jesus is the Christ, the Son of God who died for us so that we might receive God's salvation and the promise of eternal life. Thus, the message of the Gospel of John is about being saved.

The dispute about whether the Bible identifies Jesus as God centers mostly on the Gospel of John. This was made evident at the beginning of the Arian Controversy when Bishop Alexander of Egypt wrote letters condemning Arius's teaching on this subject. For biblical support, the bishop cited texts mostly from the Gospel of John. In so doing, he reflected the common, yet mistaken, viewpoint held by traditionalists and historical-critical scholars alike ever since—that this gospel identifies Jesus as God. In fact, in the second century, many Christians dismissed the Gospel of John as not God-inspired because the Gnostics liked it, thinking it presented Jesus as nonhuman.

Scholars call this supposed divergence between a human Jesus in the Synoptics and a divine Christ in the Gospel of John "the riddle of Christology."[29] But this just shows how the Gospel of John has been so greatly misunderstood. There is no divine Christ in the Fourth Gospel! If there is a "riddle of Christology," it is how this gospel has been misunderstood by church fathers who claimed it says Jesus is God and added it as a prime element of the gospel. I prefer to call their addition a corruption of the gospel.

Jesus's Name Means "Yahweh Saves"

During antiquity, people often had names that had meaning. Many names of Bible heroes also contained the shortened form of God's

---

[29] E.g., Martin Hengel, *Studies in Early Christology* (Edinburgh: T.&T. Clark, 1995), xvii; cf. *The Son of God: The Origin of Christology and the History of Jewish-Hellenistic Religion* (orig. ET 1975; London: SCM/Philadelphia: Fortress, 1976), 1.

name, *yah/jah* for Yahweh, or *el* for Elohim, which is the Hebrew word for God. For instance, Elijah means "Yahweh is my God," Isaiah means "the salvation of God," Daniel means "God is my judge," Michael means "who is like God," and Elizabeth means "God's oath."

The Gospel of John is unique in repeatedly telling readers to "believe in Jesus's name" or words to that effect. For example, this gospel's prologue says of Jesus, "to all who received him, who believed in his name, he gave power to become children of God" (John 1:12; cf. 3:18). What does it mean to believe in Jesus's name? It means to believe in the meaning of his name. So what does the name Jesus mean?

Jesus's native tongue was Aramaic, a sister language of Hebrew. His name in Aramaic is Yeshua (or Yeshu), which is Joshua (or Jehoshua) in Hebrew. Regarding the etymology of Yeshua, *ye* (and *yah*) is the shortened form of God's name YHWH. It often is rendered Yahweh; but it can be Yahveh or Yehvah. Shua means "save." So, Yeshua means "Yahweh saves" or "Yahweh is salvation." Regarding Jesus of Nazareth, the meaning of his name can be paraphrased as "Yahweh saves through this man."

The Gospel of John has much information about Jesus's name. Most are quotes from Jesus himself. For instance, the Johannine Jesus said, "I have come in my Father's name" (John 5:43), referring to God's name Yahweh or Yehvah. Jesus meant that his name Yeshua contains the shortened form of Yehvah, which is *ye*. Also, Jesus said in his high-priestly prayer to God the Father, "I have made your name known to those whom you gave me" (17:6), referring to the eleven apostles. Jesus soon said, "Holy Father, protect them in your name that you have given me, so that they may be one, as we are one. While I was with them, I protected them in your name that you have given me" (vv. 11–12). Jesus added, "I made your name known to them, and I will make it known, so that the love with which you have loved me may be in them and I in them" (v. 26).

So the important thing to understand about Jesus's Aramaic name, Yeshua, is that God saves through this man. Jesus bearing God's name does not mean he is God; rather, it means God sent him to provide salvation by dying for our sins. How do we know that this is what Jesus meant when he talked about believing in his name?

Being "Born Again" Is about Being Saved

Only the Gospel of John informs that, early in Jesus's public ministry, he told a man that he needed to be "born from above." This phrase also means "born again" or "born anew." We read, "Now there was a Pharisee named Nicodemus, a leader of the Jews. He came to Jesus by night and said to him, 'Rabbi, we know that you are a teacher who has come from God, for no one can do these signs that you do unless God is with that person.' Jesus answered him, 'Very truly I tell you, no one can see the kingdom of God without being born from above'" (John 3:1–3). Jesus meant to be born of God's Spirit, an inner act resulting in spiritual renewal. Christians often call it "the new birth."

Jesus was not original in saying this, though his terminology may have been new. Moses compared this spiritual renewal to male circumcision practiced by Jews as a sign of their covenant with God. Moses meant that circumcision is not enough to be right with Yahweh their God. He exhorted the Israelites, "Circumcise then the foreskin of your heart, and do not be stubborn any longer" (Deuteronomy 10:16; cf. Acts 7:51).

This new heart that signifies spiritual renewal applies even more to the world to come. The prophet Jeremiah said, "The days are surely coming, says the LORD, when I will make a new covenant with the house of Israel and the house of Judah. ... I will put my law within them, and I will write it on their hearts, and I will be their God, and they shall be my people" (Jeremiah 31:31, 33). And the prophet Ezekiel likewise said on God's behalf, "I will sprinkle clean water upon you, and you shall be clean from all your uncleanness. ... A new heart I will give you, and a new spirit I will put within you; and I will remove from your body the heart of stone and give you a heart of flesh. I will put my spirit within you, and make you follow my statutes ... and you shall be my people, and I will be your God. I will save you from all your uncleanness" (Ezekiel 36:25–29).

So, God giving Jews a new heart is the same as being born again. We know from the New Testament that God is going to give not only Jews but also Gentiles this new heart. Like Moses, Jesus said this change of heart should begin spiritually in this life.

Jesus told Nicodemus exactly how to be born again in this life. He said, referring to himself as the Son of Man, "And just as Moses lifted up the serpent in the wilderness, so must the Son of Man be lifted up, that whoever believes in him may have eternal life" (John 3:14). What did Jesus mean about Moses lifting a serpent? Sounds dangerous!

During the Israelites' exodus, poisonous snakes slithered into their camp. Many people were bitten and died. Moses prayed, and God told him what to do. We read, "So Moses made a serpent of bronze and put it upon a pole, and whenever a serpent bit someone, that person would look at the serpent of bronze and live" (Numbers 21:9).

When Jesus told Nicodemus, "So must the Son of Man be lifted up," he referred to his impending crucifixion and its meaning. That is, just as Moses lifted the serpent on a pole, and snake-bitten Israelites who looked at it were healed, when Jesus would be lifted onto a cross to die for the sins of others, people who believe this about him will be saved and inherit eternal life. The Johannine Jesus later explained, "And I, when I am lifted up from the earth, will draw all people to myself" (John 12:32). One way this has happened has been the pop-cultural image of a cross, often thought to refer to Jesus.

Believing God Sent Jesus Is Enough to Be Saved

The Gospel of John is unique by presenting Jesus declaring twenty-seven times that God the Father "sent me," whereas this occurs only twice in the Synoptics. The Johannine Jesus even says this as a sole faith requirement for salvation. He said, "Very truly, I tell you, anyone who hears my word and believes him who sent me has eternal life and does not come under judgment but has passed from death to life" (John 5:24). And he said, "This is the work of God, that you believe in him whom he has sent" (6:29).

I tell more about this in *The Restitution* (pp. 297–98) as follows:

> Actually, the foremost christological motif in the Fourth Gospel is not incarnation Christology but "agent Christology." John informs us no less than forty times that the Father "sent" Jesus or did "send" Him as His agent. Some have labeled this concept a "Sending Christology." Jesus claimed similarly, that He "came" or did "come" from the Father. J.A.T. Robinson explains concerning this abundant data, "The picture which John presents is of Jesus as the Father's agent."[30]
>
> To rightly understand the Johannine Jesus, Agent Christology can hardly be overemphasized. It is the corrective to the misinterpretation of some Johannine texts in which Jesus is wrongly depicted as God or as God becoming a man.
>
> Moreover, John portrays Jesus as teaching that Agent Christology, i.e., Sending Christology, should be the primary focus of saving faith for the believer.

---

[30] John A.T. Robinson, *The Priority of John*, 350. Robinson cites other scholars who so affirm.

One might ask, "How can believing that God sent Jesus be enough to be saved?" Jesus was crucified and died. If God sent Jesus, then he sent him to be crucified and die. So believing that God sent Jesus means believing God sent Jesus to the cross. Jesus told his apostles privately and clearly on three separate occasions that religious authorities at Jerusalem would kill him, and then he would rise from the dead on the third day.[31]

Obeying Jesus Is Enough to Be Saved

The Johannine literature of the New Testament has a theme, often ignored, about obeying Jesus as the sole requirement to be saved. It emerges in the Fourth Gospel in its two episodes in which Jesus was accused of claiming to be God (John 5:18–47; 10:30–38). In both episodes, Jesus makes a denial that many have misunderstood.

In the first episode, Jesus healed a man on the Sabbath. Jesus's opponents alleged that this "work" violated the Sabbath (John 5:1–16). He denied this accusation by saying, "My Father is still working, and I also am working" (v. 17). He meant God heals on the Sabbath, so it cannot be a violation if he does too. John adds, "For this reason the Jews were seeking all the more to kill him, because he was not only breaking the sabbath, but was also calling God his own Father, thereby making himself equal to God" (v. 18). This verse has been widely misunderstood as being the author's assessment. On the contrary, the author presents this as the viewpoint of Jesus's opponents. For, Jesus then denies this accusation with a lengthy rebuttal in vv. 19–47. He begins it by saying, "Very truly I tell you, the Son can do nothing on his own, but only what he sees the Father doing" (v. 19, cf. 30). This is a clear denial that he is God. He then says, "Those who have done good" will arise from the dead "to the resurrection of life, and those who have done evil to the resurrection of condemnation" (v. 29).

The author of 1 John teaches similarly. He says of Jesus, "We may be sure that we know him, if we obey his commandments. Whoever says, 'I have come to know him,' but does not obey his commandments, is a liar, and in such a person the truth does not exist" (1 John 2:3–4). The author adds, "Everyone who does right has been born of him" (1 John 2:29), resulting in them being "children of God" (3:1).

Jesus often taught this theme—about living righteously as evidence of being born again—starting with his Sermon on the

---

[31] See Matthew 16:21; 17:22–23; 20:18–19; Mark 8:31; 9:31; 10:33–34; Luke 9:22; 18:31–33; cf. 9:44.

Mount. Its beatitudes reveal that people will be blessed for being penitent, mournful, meek, merciful, pure in heart, peaceful, and living righteously (Matthew 5:3–10). He explained, "For I tell you, unless your righteousness exceeds that of the scribes and Pharisees, you will never enter the kingdom of heaven" (v. 20). Jesus also said therein that at the judgment many will address him as "Lord," yet he will say to them, "I never knew you; go away from me, you evildoers" (7:23).

Some may think this emphasis on righteous living clashes with Paul's teaching on justification by faith. No so. When Paul writes negatively about "works of the law" (e.g., Romans 3:20, 28), he often means ritual. This is what "the new perspective on Paul" is about, a term coined by James D. G. Dunn. Paul taught salvation comes only by faith, but he often explained that faith produces some evidence of righteous living or else it is pseudo-faith.[32] Paul explains, "The one who is righteous will live by faith" (Romans 1:17). He explains, as does Jesus and much of the New Testament, that the judgment will be based on deeds (2:6–10; cf. Revelation 20:11–12). Paul also says that the Holy Spirit empowers believers to live righteously. He later wrote about those who "profess to know God, but they deny him by their actions" (Titus 1:16). Thus, Paul does not conflict with James's famous statement: "A person is justified by works and not by faith alone. ... faith without works is also dead" (James 2:24, 26). Real faith produces good works.

Therefore, attaining God's salvation simply by believing God sent Jesus and following Jesus is propositionally more minimalist than the Gospel of John has been generally understood.

Jesus Being the Son of God Does Not Mean He Is God

We considered Jesus's Sonship in Chapter 4. But he is called "the Son (of God)" far more in John's gospel than in the Synoptics. In one instance Jesus identified himself as "God's Son." It was when Jews wrongly accused him, "'You, though only a human being, are making yourself God.' Jesus answered ... 'I said, "I am God's Son"'" (John 10:33–34, 36). Jesus distinguished between God and his own identity as God's Son. In doing so, he denied that he claimed to be God. It seems his interlocutors accepted this denial by not arguing further. They knew that being God's Son is not the same as being God.

As in the Synoptics, this gospel reports an incident in which the titles Messiah and Son of God are used synonymously, indicating Son of

---

[32] E.g., 1 Corinthians 6:9–11; Galatians 5:19–21; Ephesians 5:5–6; Titus 1:16.

God does not mean Jesus is God. It is when Jesus was about to raise his deceased friend Lazarus from the dead. Jesus said to Martha, Lazarus's sister, "I am the resurrection and the life" (John 11:25). Martha replied, "Yes, Lord, I believe that you are the Messiah, the Son of God, the one coming into the world" (v. 27). As here, so much New Testament evidence exists showing that identifying Jesus as the Son of God does not mean he is God.

Most Johannine scholars insist that the Fourth Evangelist concludes his book in John 20:30–31, so that John 21 is an addendum. Regardless, John 20:30–31 reads as follows: "Now Jesus did many other signs in the presence of his disciples that are not written in this book. But these are written so that you may continue to believe that Jesus is the Messiah, the Son of God, and that through believing you may have life in his name." To have "life in his name" refers to the promise of eternal life, which is what the Christian gospel is about. This author identifying Jesus as the Messiah, the Son of God, is part of the gospel. He seems to use these epithets synonymously.

Furthermore, John 20:30–31 reveals the author's purpose for writing his gospel. It is that readers "may continue to believe Jesus is the Messiah, the Son of God." This strongly suggests it was not the author's purpose in writing his gospel to declare Jesus is God as many have thought because of the traditional translation of John 1:1c, "the Word was God." Saying Jesus is God would have been far greater status than what the Fourth Evangelist does say is his purpose—to show that Jesus is the Messiah, the Son of God.

Despite John's prologue, his gospel repeatedly shows that people questioned who Jesus was, mostly if he was the Messiah. We see this with the Samaritan woman at the well (John 4:25–26), Jesus at the Feast of Booths (7:26, 31, 41–43; 8:25, 53; 9:22), Jesus with Martha (John 11:27), and during Passion Week (John 12:13–15, 34). There is no inquiry about whether Jesus is God. All this evidence suggests that the prologue does not say Jesus is God.

Now, we should not think the Johannine literature only requires faith in Jesus as Messiah, the Son of God, without also necessitating faith in his sacrificial death for our sins as Savior. For 1 John twice says "Jesus Christ" is "the atoning sacrifice for our sins" (1 John 2:2; 4:10). The Hebrew word *mashiach*, meaning "anointed (one)," is translated Messiah. God's anointing was often depicted by pouring oil on a recipient whom God had chosen and called to do a special task. Israel always performed such a ceremony when installing a king or priest.

Identifying Jesus as *mashiach*—translated *christos* in Greek—means God anointed him for the task of dying for our sins. And after that, in heaven, he will be crowned king and be given his kingdom to bring to earth at his second coming (cf. Daniel 7:13–14). Finally, in all those Johannine texts that inform about Jesus being the Messiah, the Son of God, nothing is said about him being God.

The Johannine Jesus Had a God—the Father "Almighty"

Three times Isaiah presents the righteous, suffering servant of Yahweh as saying "my God" (Isaiah 49:4–5; 61:1). Christians believe this servant was Messiah Jesus. The prophet Micah does likewise by first prophesying that the Messiah would be born in "Bethlehem" and become "one who is to rule in Israel ... in the majesty of the name of the LORD his God" (Micah 5:2, 4). So rather than *being God*, Messiah *has a God*.

The Johannine Jesus sometimes continued this Old Testament tradition by calling God the Father "my God." For instance, we read that when the resurrected Jesus appeared to Mary Magdalene at the tomb on Easter morning, "Jesus said to her ... 'go to my brothers and say to them, "I am ascending to my Father and your Father, to my God and your God"'" (John 20:17). Since this saying appears near Thomas's confession, "My Lord and my God" in v. 28, the traditionalists' interpretation that Thomas here calls Jesus "my God" seems to conflict with Jesus calling the Father "my God."

The book of Revelation, which scholars categorize as Johannine literature, has seven messages by the heavenly Jesus that were sent to seven churches (Revelation 2—3). In only one verse, Jesus calls God the Father "my God" four times (3:12). Jesus tells each of these churches that if they "conquer" sin and temptation, they will be greatly rewarded. He then cites himself as the model, saying, "To the one who conquers I will give a place with me on my throne [on earth], just as I myself conquered and sat down with my Father on his throne" in heaven (3:21).

Christians sometimes ask me, "What benefit is gained by believing Jesus is only our Lord and Savior but not God?" I usually answer by explaining that we should think of Jesus as a conqueror who overcame sin and temptation to qualify to die for our sins as God's sinless, sacrificial "lamb without defect or blemish" (1 Peter 1:19). So, as a man Jesus had to persevere to become our model overcomer. Yet many Trinitarians admit that, according to their theology, it could not have been a struggle for Jesus, even in his temptations by the devil (Matthew 4:11), since he was God and "God cannot be tempted by evil" (James 1:13). But if Jesus's temptations were real, that proves he was not God.

We also should understand that believing Jesus is fully God, thus equal to God the Father in every sense, results in a reduction of the Father's superiority and majesty. The Johannine Jesus made this clear when he said, "The Father is greater than I" (John 14:28). If Jesus is equal to the Father, the Father cannot be the Almighty. The book of Revelation (Apocalypse) uniquely identifies God as "the Almighty" (Gr. *ho pantokrator*) nine times.[33] Jesus is never called "the Almighty" in the Bible. In sum, patristic theology diminishes the identities of God as the Almighty and Jesus as the Overcomer.

Agent Christology

The Gospel of John is unique in presenting Jesus as God's agent par excellence. Johannine texts commonly misunderstood to mean Jesus *is* God really mean God was *in* Jesus, which is not the same. In other words, *God was in Christ, not Christ was God*. I related this truth in Chapter 1 about Jesus teaching the apostles Philip and Thomas the mutual indwelling of the Father and the Son (cf. John 10:38). Jesus said to them two times in short compass, "I am in the Father and the Father is in me" (John 14:10–11). I believe that is what Thomas meant days later when he saw and heard the risen Jesus and then said to him, "My Lord and my God" (John 20:28). By saying to Jesus "my God," Thomas meant what his Master had told him days earlier, "the Father is in me." This truth about Jesus is called Agent Christology. That is, with the Father indwelling the Son, Jesus represented God so completely that it was as though God was there.

God the Father Is "The Only True God"

The foremost text in the Bible that refutes the notion that Jesus is God is in the Gospel of John, and it was uttered by Jesus himself. It appears in Jesus's so-called "high-priestly prayer" recorded only in this gospel. Jesus said it right before his arrest, trial, and crucifixion. Judas had left the supper, perhaps an hour or two earlier, to betray the Master. We read of Jesus, "He looked up to heaven and said, 'Father,

---

[33] Revelation 1:8; 4:8; 11:17; 15:3; 16:7, 14; 19:6, 15; 21:22. Two have *tou pantokratopos*.

the hour has come, glorify your Son so that the Son may glorify you, since you have given him authority over all people, to give eternal life to all whom you have given him. And this is eternal life, that they may know you, the only true God, and Jesus Christ, whom you have sent'" (John 17:1–3; cf. 5:44). Thus, Jesus called God the Father "the only true God," and in doing so he distinguished this God from himself.

Folks, it doesn't get any clearer than that! And this saying of Jesus, about God the Father being "the only true God," appears only in the Gospel of John. This gospel says Jesus revealed most succinctly that he is not God and that only the Father is God.

Chapter 6
The Gospel According to the Acts of the Apostles

The fifth book in the New Testament is The Acts of the Apostles. It relates what scholars call the Jesus Movement that developed after Jesus arose from the dead and ascended to heaven (Acts 1:9–11). His apostles and other disciples went about spreading the "good news," the gospel (Gr. *euangelion*) about Jesus mentioned often in Acts.

There are twenty-four messages in this "book of Acts" as it is often called.[34] They are evangelistic proclamations of the gospel or summary fragments thereof. The first several speeches are mostly by Peter, and the rest are by Paul. Four are defenses that Peter and then Paul gave before authorities after they were arrested for preaching the gospel. Only four messages were spoken by other disciples (Acts 6:5; 7:2–53; 8:4–40). *These messages in Acts may be the strongest evidence in the New Testament which shows that church fathers erred in later adding to the gospel that Jesus is God.*[35]

Luke's Introduction in His Book of Acts

The book of Acts seems to have been written by Luke, a ministry companion of Paul.[36] He wrote it for Theophilus, who may have been his patron. Luke begins by citing his Gospel of Luke. "In the first book, Theophilus, I wrote about all that Jesus began to do and teach until the day when he was taken up to heaven" (Acts 1:1–2). Then Luke backtracks by saying of Jesus and "the apostles whom he had chosen" (v. 2), "After his suffering he presented himself alive to them by many convincing proofs, appearing to them for forty days and speaking about the kingdom of God" (v. 3). So from the very beginning of the book of Acts, Luke highlights Jesus's resurrection. This central theme continues throughout the book of Acts as the preeminent element of the gospel.

---

[34] Martin Dibelius (*Studies in the Acts of the Apostles* [London: SCM, 1956], 150) counts twenty-four speeches.

[35] *The Restitution* does not have a chapter on Acts, so it treats Acts lightly.

[36] E.g., Colossians 4:14; 2 Timothy 4:11. Luke's constant "we" in Acts indicates his inclusion.

Luke then reports that Jesus gathered his eleven apostles on Mount Olivet, which overlooked Jerusalem and its temple. He gave them instructions to remain in Jerusalem to be empowered by the Holy Spirit (Acts 1:4–8). Then we read, "When he had said this, as they were watching, he was lifted up and a cloud took him out of their sight" (v. 9). Two angels then appeared, saying, "Men of Galilee, why do you stand looking up toward heaven? This Jesus, who has been taken up from you into heaven, will come in the same way as you saw him go into heaven" (v. 11), referring to Jesus's second coming.

Luke next relates that the apostles and others, about 120, were together in what may have been the Upper Room where Jesus and his apostles ate the Last Supper (Acts 1:13, 15). Luke says Peter announced that Judas's betrayal of Jesus had been predicted in Scripture (vv. 16–20). He gave this quotation, "Let another take his position of overseer" (v. 20; cf. Psalm 109:8). Peter continued, "So one of the men who have accompanied us during all the time that the Lord Jesus went in and out among us, beginning from the baptism of John until the day when he was taken up from us—one of these must become a witness with us to his resurrection'" (vv. 21–22). Luke adds, "And they cast lots for them, and the lot fell on Matthias, and he was added to the eleven apostles" (v. 26). Here we see that the two requirements for Judas's replacement were that Matthias had participated in Jesus's public ministry from its start and had seen the risen Jesus. Again, Jesus's resurrection is important in the beginning of Acts, even in choosing Judas's replacement.

The Evangelistic Messages in Acts

We must now ask—what is this good news called "the gospel" in the book of Acts? We will notice that *none of these evangelistic speeches in Acts proclaim that Jesus is God or indicate an incarnation in which he came down from heaven to become a man*. To prove this, we will examine all that they say about Jesus. As we do, we will discover that the central point of most of these speeches is Jesus's literal resurrection from the dead. It is mentioned eighteen times in these twenty-four messages, and the general resurrection is mentioned four times (all colored in gray), as the following reveal:[37]

1. **Peter's First, Pentecostal Sermon**: "Jesus of Nazareth, a man attested to you by God with deeds of power, wonders, and

---

[37] Phrases about Jesus's resurrection are identified in gray color.

signs that God did through him among you ... you crucified and killed. ... But God raised him up, having released him from the agony of death" (2:22–24). Peter then quotes Psalm 16:10 twice (vv. 27, 31), about Jesus's body not experiencing corruption. Peter saying Jesus is "a man" who depended on God to do these works through him indicates Jesus is not God (cf. John 5:19, 30).

2. **Peter's Second Sermon**: "Jesus, whom you handed over and rejected in the presence of Pilate, though he had decided to release him. .... And you killed the author of life, whom God raised from the dead. ... Repent, therefore, and turn to God so that your sins may be wiped out" (3:13, 15, 19). So, Peter was "proclaiming that in Jesus there is the resurrection of the dead" (4:2).

3. **Peter Before the Elders and Rulers**: "Jesus Christ of Nazareth, whom you crucified, whom God raised from the dead. .... There is salvation in no one else ... among mortals by which we must be saved" (4:10–11).

4. **Luke Summarizes What Has Happened**: "With great power the apostles gave their testimony to the resurrection of the Lord Jesus" (4:33).

5. **Peter before the Sanhedrin at Jerusalem**: "Then the high priest took action; he and all who were with him (that is, the sect of the Sadducees), being filled with jealousy, arrested the apostles and put them in the public prison. ... The high priest questioned them, saying, 'We gave you strict orders not to teach in this name' ... But Peter and the apostles answered, 'We must obey God rather than any human authority. The God of our ancestors raised up Jesus, whom you had killed by hanging him on a tree. God exalted him at his right hand as Leader and Savior that he might give repentance to Israel and forgiveness of sins. And we are witnesses of these things'" (5:17-18, 27, 29–32).

6. **Luke Summarizes Again**: "As they left the council, they rejoiced. ... And every day in the temple and at home they did not cease to teach and proclaim Jesus as the Messiah" (5:41–42). "Proclaim" translates *euangelizomenoi* in the Greek text (cf. 11:20). So, they proclaimed this gospel to Jews in Jerusalem.

7. **Stephen Martyred**: Jewish opponents of deacon Stephen brought him before the Sanhedrin for interrogation. His recorded speech, in Acts 7:2–53, is the longest in the New Testament by a disciple of Jesus. He recounts the history of Israel and then

declares to this council that had charged Jesus with blasphemy and pressured the Romans to crucify him, "You stiff-necked people, uncircumcised in heart and ears, you are forever opposing the Holy Spirit" (Acts 7:51). Luke afterward relates, "But filled with the Holy Spirit, he gazed into heaven and saw the glory of God and Jesus standing at the right hand of God. 'Look,' he said, 'I see the heavens opened and the Son of Man standing at the right hand of God!' But they covered their ears, and with a loud shout all rushed against him. Then they dragged him out of the city and began to stone him" (vv. 55–58). This is the only occurrence in the New Testament in which a disciple of Jesus identified him as "the Son of Man." The young and unconverted Saul/Paul was there watching and "approved of their killing him" (8:1).

8. **Philip at Samaria**: "Philip went down to the city of Samaria and proclaimed the Messiah to them. .... They believed Philip, who was proclaiming the good news about the kingdom of God and the name of Jesus Christ" (8:5, 12). Peter and John came there from Jerusalem to impart the Holy Spirit to them. We then read, "After Peter and John had testified and spoken the word of the Lord, they returned to Jerusalem, proclaiming the good news to many villages of the Samaritans" (v. 25).

9. **Philip to the Ethiopian Eunuch**: "Now there was an Ethiopian eunuch, court official of ... the queen of the Ethiopians. ... He had come to Jerusalem to worship, and was returning home; seated in his chariot, he was reading the prophet Isaiah. ... he invited Philip to get in and sit beside him. ... Philip began to speak, and starting with this scripture he proclaimed to him the good news about Jesus" (8:27, 31, 35).

10. **Paul's Conversion on the Road to Damascus**: "For several days he was with the disciples in Damascus, and immediately he began to proclaim Jesus in the synagogues, saying, 'He is the Son of God.' ... and confounded the Jews who lived in Damascus by proving that Jesus was the Messiah" (9:19–20, 22).

11. **Peter in the Household of Cornelius**: Peter preached to Cornelius's household, "God anointed Jesus of Nazareth with the Holy Spirit and with power; how he went about doing good and healing all who were oppressed by the devil, for God was with him. ... They put him to death by hanging him on a tree, but God raised him up on the third day and allowed him to appear, not to all the people but to us who were chosen by God as witnesses

and who ate and drank with him after he rose from the dead'" (10:38–41). Jesus needing the Spirit and God with him indicates he is not God.

12. **Paul at Antioch, Pisidia**: "God has brought to Israel a Savior, Jesus. ... Even though they found no cause for a sentence of death, they asked Pilate to have him killed. When they had carried out everything that was written about him, they took him down from the tree and laid him in a tomb. But God raised him from the dead, and for many days he appeared to those who came up with him from Galilee to Jerusalem, and they are now his witnesses to the people. And we bring you the good news that what God has promised to our ancestors he has fulfilled for us, their children, by raising Jesus. ... As to his raising him from the dead, no more to return to corruption, he has spoken in this way ... 'You will not let your Holy One experience corruption'" (13:23, 28–33, 35).

13. **Paul and Silas at Philippi**: While Paul and Silas were in prison in Philippi, "Suddenly, there was an earthquake ... and immediately all the doors were opened and everyone's chains were unfastened. ... The jailor ... fell down trembling before Paul and Silas. Then he brought them outside and said, 'Sirs, what must I do to be saved?' They answered them, 'Believe in the Lord Jesus, and you will be saved, you and your household'" (16:26, 29–31).

14. **Paul at Thessalonica**: "Paul and Silas ... came to Thessalonica, where there was a Jewish synagogue. And Paul went in, as was his custom, and on three Sabbath days argued with them from the scriptures, explaining and proving that it was necessary for the Messiah to suffer and to rise from the dead and saying, 'This is the Messiah, Jesus whom I am proclaiming to you'" (17:1–3).

15. **Paul at Athens**: "Paul was ... deeply distressed to see that the city was full of idols. So he argued in the synagogue with the Jews and the devout persons and also in the marketplace every day with those who happened to be there. ... He was telling the good news about Jesus and the resurrection" (17:16–18).

16. **Paul at The Areopagus**: At Athens, in synagogue and marketplace, Paul "was telling the good news about Jesus and the resurrection" (17:18). "So they took him and brought him to the Areopagus and asked him, 'May we know what this new teaching is that you are presenting?'" (v. 19). Paul answered, "'The God who made the world and everything in it, he is Lord of heaven

and earth ... He has fixed a day on which he will have the world judged in righteousness by a man whom he has appointed, and of this he has given assurance to all by raising him from the dead.' When they heard of the resurrection of the dead, some scoffed, but others said, 'We will hear you again about this.' At that point Paul left them. But some of them joined him and became believers" (vv. 24, 31–34).

17. **Paul at Corinth**: "Paul left Athens and went to Corinth. .... Every Sabbath he would argue in the synagogue and would try to convince Jews and Greeks. ... Paul was occupied with proclaiming the word, testifying to Jews that the Messiah was Jesus" (18:1, 4–5).

18. **Apollos at Ephesus**: "Now there came to Ephesus a Jew named Apollos, a native of Alexandria. He was an eloquent man, well-versed in the scriptures. ... He powerfully refuted the Jews in public, showing by the scriptures that the Messiah is Jesus" (18:24, 28).

19. **Paul at Ephesus**: "Paul passed through the interior regions and came to Ephesus, where he found some disciples" who only knew of John's baptism. "Paul said, 'John baptized with the baptism of repentance, telling the people to believe in the one who was to come after him, that is, in Jesus.' On hearing this, they were baptized in the name of the Lord Jesus. ... He entered the synagogue and for three months spoke out boldly and argued persuasively about the kingdom of God" (19:1, 4–5, 8).

20. **Paul's Farewell to the Elders of Ephesus**: Paul asked the elders of the church at Ephesus to meet with him. Luke informs, "When they came to him, he said to them: 'You yourselves know how I lived among you. ... I did not shrink from doing anything helpful, proclaiming the message to you and teaching you publicly and from house to house, as I testified to both Jews and Greeks about repentance toward God and faith toward our Lord Jesus. ... And now I know that none of you, among whom I have gone about proclaiming the kingdom, will ever see my face again. ... Keep watch over yourselves and over the flock, of which the Holy Spirit has made you overseers, to shepherd the church of God that he obtained with the blood of his own Son'" (20:18, 20–21, 25, 28).

21. **Paul's Defense Before the Sanhedrin**: "Brothers, I am a Pharisee, a son of Pharisees. I am on trial concerning the hope of the resurrection of the dead" (22:6).

22. **Paul's Defense Before Governor Felix**: "When the governor motioned to him to speak, Paul replied: ... 'I admit to you, that according to the Way, which they call a sect, I worship the God of our ancestors, believing everything laid down according to the law or written in the prophets. I have a hope in God—a hope that they themselves also accept—that there will be a resurrection of both the righteous and the unrighteous. Therefore I do my best always to have a clear conscience toward God and all people. Now after some years I came to bring alms to my people and to offer sacrifices. While I was doing this, they found me in the temple. ... Let these men here tell what crime they had found when I stood before the council, unless it was this one sentence that I called out while standing before them, "It is about the resurrection of the dead that I am on trial before you today"'" (24:10, 14–17, 20–21).

23. **Paul's Defense Before King Agrippa**: Governor Festus spoke to King Agrippa about the Jews having gotten Paul imprisoned, saying the Jews "had certain points of disagreement with him about their religion and about a certain Jesus, who had died but whom Paul asserted to be alive. ... Agrippa said to Festus, 'I would like to hear the man myself.' 'Tomorrow,' he said, 'you will hear him'" (25:19, 22). "Agrippa said to Paul, 'You have permission to speak for yourself.' Then Paul stretched out his hand and began to defend himself: 'I consider myself fortunate that it is before you, King Agrippa, I am to make my defense today against all the accusations of the Jews, because you are especially familiar with all the customs and controversies of the Jews ... And now I stand here on trial on account of my hope in the promise made by God to our ancestors. ... It is for this hope, Your Excellency, that I am accused by Jews! Why is it thought incredible by any of you that God raises the dead? ... I ... declared ... that they should repent and turn to God and do deeds consistent with repentance. For this reason the Jews seized me in the temple and tried to kill me. To this day I have had help from God, and so I stand here, testifying to both small and great, saying nothing but what the prophets and Moses said would take place: that the Messiah must suffer and that, by being the first to rise from the dead, he would proclaim light both to our people and to the gentiles'" (26:1–3, 6–8, 19–23).

24. **Paul at Rome**: "When we came into Rome, Paul was allowed to live by himself. ... He called together the local leaders of the

Jews. When they had assembled he said to them, 'Brothers, though I had done nothing against our people or the customs of our ancestors, yet I was arrested in Jerusalem and handed over to the Romans. ... I was compelled to appeal to the emperor. ... For this reason therefore I asked to see you and speak with you, since it is for the sake of the hope of Israel that I am bound with this chain.' They replied, 'We have received no letters from Judea about you. ... But we would like to hear from you what you think, for with regard to this sect we know that everywhere it is spoken against.' ... From morning until evening he explained the matter to them, testifying to the kingdom of God and trying to convince them about Jesus both from the law of Moses and from the prophets" (28:16–17, 19–23).

Jesus's Resurrection Is Central to the Gospel in Acts

To repeat, these twenty-four evangelistic speeches in Acts tell of the resurrection of Jesus eighteen times. That is way more than anything else mentioned in these texts about Jesus. The next most repeated mention about Jesus in these messages is that he is the Messiah of Israel, which is stated eight times. Furthermore, in Paul's three defenses of himself reported in Acts—before the Sanhedrin, Governor Felix, and King Agrippa—he mentions the general resurrection of the dead four times. Yet Paul does so by relating it to Jesus's resurrection. Clearly, *Jesus's resurrection from the dead is by far the core of these twenty-four evangelistic speeches in the book of Acts.* While the speakers tailored their messages to their audiences, they usually included Jesus's resurrection. Identifying Jesus as the Messiah was proclaimed to Jews but rarely to Gentiles. Why? The Messiah was to be the king of Israel, which would not be so relevant to Gentiles.

Why is Jesus's resurrection so prominent in these evangelistic messages in Acts? It is the power of God demonstrated among humans like nothing that has ever occurred in this world before or since. Jesus's resurrection from the dead makes Christianity unique among the world's religions. And it is why Luke says the Jewish opponents of Paul and Silas at Thessalonica had exclaimed, "These people who have been turning the world upside down have come here" (Acts 17:6). Indeed, they came to the synagogue and they "argued with them from the scriptures, explaining and proving that it was necessary for the Messiah to suffer and to rise from the dead" (vv. 2–3). I am of the strong opinion that *if Jesus had not risen from the dead, there never would have been any Christianity. And if Jesus is not the promised Messiah, Israel will never have such a Messiah.*

Some shortsighted Christians have argued that the miracle of Jesus's resurrection from the dead indicates he was God. But if that were true, all believers who will be raised from the dead at the end of this age will be Gods/gods too, which is ludicrous! Similarly, some Christians have asserted that Jesus performing miracles during his ministry show he was God. But if that were true, many Old Testament prophets and apostles of Jesus who did miracles would have to be Gods/gods as well.

Finally, I think we can trust that Luke provides reasonably accurate summaries of these messages in Acts. In the introduction to his gospel, he explains that the traditions about Jesus that he reports therein came from "eyewitnesses and servants of the word" and that he "investigated everything carefully" to "know the truth" (Luke 1:2–3).

Conclusion

My dear friend Jimmy Dunn (now deceased) observed of these gospel speeches in the book of Acts, "the very marked primitiveness of the Christology" is "not characteristic of the heightened Christology of subsequent years."[38] Indeed!

It is astonishing to read these evangelistic speeches in the book of Acts that were proclaimed by the early Christians and realize that ever since the fourth century Christians have declared that the most important proposition about Jesus's identity is that *he is God* and that a person must believe this to become a Christian, that is, to be forgiven of their sins, receive God's salvation, and inherit eternal life. Yet, *Jesus is never identified as God in these evangelistic messages in the book of Acts.* If Jesus was God, and those early disciples knew it, they surely would have included in their gospel messages what would have been *far greater news.* I state in *The Restitution* (p. 222):

> The book of Acts reveals that the early Christians made Jesus's resurrection the chief cornerstone of their kerygma. They never preached that Jesus was God but that God raised Jesus from the dead and that they were witnesses of it by afterwards having seen the risen Jesus (e.g., Acts 3:15). Subsequent church fathers reversed this early church kerygma, asserting that the foundation of Christian faith was

---

[38] James D. G. Dunn, *Christianity in the Making*, 3 vols., *Beginning from Jerusalem* (Grand Rapids: Eerdmans, 2009), 2:93, 95.

that Jesus Christ was God. In so doing, they made Jesus's resurrection a secondary element in their kerygma.

So, you Nicene and post-Nicene church fathers, this God-inspired evidence in The Acts of the Apostles shows that you guys were *freakin' crazy* to usurp the authority of Jesus's apostles by adding to their gospel about their Lord Jesus Christ, boldly declaring he was and is God and demanding that people must believe this to be saved, that is, to be a genuine Christian. *The book of Acts reveals without a shadow of a doubt that you church fathers corrupted the gospel.*

Chapter 7
The Gospel According to Paul

The apostle Paul was both an astute theologian and an evangelistic preacher. He traveled about much of the Roman Empire, planting churches and ministering to them. His usual practice was to enter a city and first attend its synagogue on the Sabbath. He especially tried to persuade Jews that Jesus is Israel's promised Messiah. Yet, although Paul was a Jew, God called him to become "an apostle to the Gentiles" (Romans 11:13; cf. Galatians 1:8–9). Again, Jesus being Israel's Messiah was rather irrelevant to Gentiles.

Paul wrote many letters that comprise one-fourth of the New Testament. In them, he often writes about "the gospel," sometimes even calling it "my gospel" (Romans 2:16; 16:25; 2 Timothy 2:8). In it, Paul says to both Jews and Gentiles that Jesus died on the cross for our sins, and God raised him from the dead. These two points were the primary elements of Paul's gospel.

If we could ask Paul if Jesus preexisted as God and then came down from heaven to become a man, and if we could ask Paul if God is three coequal and coeternal Persons, I believe this great man of God and accomplished theologian would have gotten a perplexed look on his face and said something like this: *"What are you guys talking about?"* He might have added, *"God becoming a man? That's paganism!"*

Paul's Gospel in Acts

We have seen that the book of Acts consists of historical narratives about the early Christians spreading the gospel. The first few chapters are mostly about the apostle Peter doing this as the foremost apostle to the Jews. The remainder of the book of Acts is mostly about Paul and his associates traveling about the Roman Empire, proclaiming the gospel to some Jews but especially to Gentiles. For instance, early in his mission, "Paul left Athens and went to Corinth.... Paul was occupied with proclaiming the word, testifying to the Jews that the Messiah was Jesus. When they opposed and reviled him, in protest he shook the dust from his clothes and said to them ... 'From now on I will go to the Gentiles'" (Acts 18:1, 5).

So he did. We have seen that a Gentile jailer in Philippi asked the imprisoned Paul and Silas, his associate, "'Sirs, what must I do to be saved?' They answered, 'Believe in the Lord Jesus, and you will be saved, you and your household'" (Acts 16:30–31). Believe what? Luke had just informed, "After midnight, Paul and Silas were praying and singing hymns to God, and the prisoners were listening to them" (v. 25). The jailer likely was too. Their hymns may have included the message of Jesus's death and resurrection. Being saved is what Paul's gospel was all about—being saved by believing in Jesus.

We next read in Acts that Paul and Silas traveled to "Thessalonica, where there was a synagogue of the Jews. And Paul went in as was his custom, and on three sabbath days argued with them from the scriptures, explaining and proving that it was necessary for the Messiah to suffer and to rise from the dead" (Acts 17:1–3). Jews certainly did not think the Messiah would be killed; rather, they expected from their Scriptures that he would deliver Israel from its enemies and make it the greatest nation on earth. They did not understand from Scripture that for Messiah, the cross must come before the crown.

So, we again see that Paul's gospel consisted of three primary elements: (1) Jesus is Messiah and Lord, (2) he suffered a crucifixion death for our sins, and (3) God raised him from the dead. Nothing here about Jesus being God or having an incarnation.

Also at Thessalonica, Paul and Silas soon encountered opposition from Jews. They formed a mob and caused an uproar in the marketplace, shouting, "These people who have been turning the world upside down have come here also, ... saying that there is another king named Jesus" (Acts 17:6–7). We next read, "That very night the believers sent Paul and Silas to Beronea" (v. 10). There, "Jews were more receptive than those in Thessalonica, for they welcomed the message very eagerly and examined the scriptures every day to see whether these things were so" (v. 11). What things? It seems to have been the three elements of Paul's gospel message cited above.

Yet Jews from Thessalonica came there and stirred up trouble again, forcing Paul to escape to Athens (Acts 17:13–15), the capital of Greece. Paul soon became engaged in a debate with some philosophers. They brought him to the famed Areopagus and asked him to expound on his teaching. Luke then records an extensive sermon Paul preached to them (vv. 22–31). We read in Chapter 6 Paul concluded, "'While God has overlooked the times of human ignorance, now he commands all people everywhere to repent, because he has fixed a day on which he will have the world judged in righteousness by a man whom he has appointed, and of this he has given assurance to all by raising him from the dead.' When they heard of the resurrection of the dead, some scoffed" (vv. 30–31). So, even to these Athenians, known for delving into philosophies and new ideas, Paul preached to them the resurrection and, more particularly, Jesus's resurrection.

Paul's Gospel in Romans

Paul's first New Testament letter is written to believers ("the saints") at Rome. Often called "the book of Romans," it is a lengthy treatise on Christian doctrine that is full of "the gospel." It begins, "Paul, a servant of Christ Jesus, called to be an apostle, set apart for the gospel of God, which he promised beforehand through his prophets in the holy scriptures, the gospel concerning his Son, who was descended from David according to the flesh and was declared to be Son of God with power according to the spirit of holiness by resurrection from the dead, Jesus Christ our Lord" (Romans 1:1–4). Paul means Jesus's resurrection affirms he is the Son of God. Paul unveils an "eagerness to proclaim the gospel" to citizens of Rome (v. 15). He explains, "For I am not ashamed of the gospel, for it is God's saving power for everyone who believes" (v. 16).

The second foremost text in Paul's letters in which he defines this gospel is in the book of Romans. He presents the requirements for receiving God's salvation by saying, "If you confess with your mouth that Jesus is Lord and believe in your heart that God raised him from the dead, you will be saved. For one believes with the heart, leading to righteousness, and one confesses with the mouth, leading to salvation" (Romans 10:9–10). At the beginning and end of Romans, Paul says the purpose of his gospel is to "bring about the obedience of faith" (Romans 1:6; 16:26), which results in salvation.

Paul assures the believers in Rome that during his missionary travels, "from Jerusalem and as far away as Illyricum I have fully proclaimed the good news of Christ" (Romans 15:19). Thus, Paul proclaimed the full gospel (Gr. *peplerokenai to euangelion*) so that there was nothing lacking in it. Paul never says in his gospel messages in his biblical corpus that Jesus is God, much less that a person must believe this for salvation. So, church fathers clearly were wrong in adding that to Paul's gospel. Their reasoning would be that Paul says Jesus is God in Romans 9:5, 2 Thessalonians 1:12, and Titus 2:13, therefore Paul's gospel says Jesus is God. Not so fast! This is why I'm saying a distinction should be made between actual gospel texts and the rest of Scripture.

Paul's Gospel in 1 Corinthians

The apostle Paul had been an early missionary to Corinth, Greece (Acts 18:1). He later wrote to the church there, about it being divided regarding teachers (1 Corinthians 1:11–13). He says, "Christ did not send me to baptize but to proclaim the gospel, and not with eloquent wisdom, so that the cross of Christ might not be emptied of its power" (v. 17). Paul further explains, "God decided, through the foolishness of our proclamation, to save those who believe" (v. 21). Believe what, that Jesus is God? No! Paul exclaims, "we proclaim Christ crucified" (v. 23). Again, one of the two core elements of Paul's gospel for the Gentiles is Jesus's crucifixion, and the other is his resurrection. Paul continues, "When I came to you, brothers and sisters, I did not come proclaiming the testimony of God to you with superior speech or wisdom. For I decided to know nothing among you except Jesus Christ and him crucified" (2:1–2). No deity of Christ or God is a Trinity.

We have already considered Jesus's institution of the communion service that would memorialize his atoning death. Paul mentions this symbol here in this letter, further indicating how central it is to his gospel message. He says, "For I received from the Lord what I also handed on to you, that the Lord Jesus on the night when he was betrayed took a loaf of bread, and when he had given thanks, he broke it and said, 'This is my body that is for you. Do this in remembrance of me.' In the same way he took the cup also, after supper, saying, 'This cup is the new covenant in my blood. Do this, as often as you drink it, in remembrance of me.' For as often as you eat this bread and drink the cup, you proclaim the Lord's death until he comes" (1 Corinthians 11:23–26).

Throughout Paul's New Testament corpus, his premier text that defines his gospel is in 1 Corinthians 15:1–5. Many scholars regard it as the preeminent definition of the gospel in the entire New Testament. It reads as follows:

> Now I want you to understand, brothers and sisters, the good news that I proclaimed to you, which you in turn received, in which also you stand, through which also you are being saved, if you hold firmly to the message that I proclaimed to you—unless you have come to believe in vain. For I handed on to you as of first importance what I in turn had received: that Christ died for our sins in accordance with the scriptures and that he was buried and that he was raised on the third day in accordance with the scriptures and that he appeared to Cephas, then to the twelve.

For Paul, the atoning death and resurrection of Jesus was the core of his message to the world, describing it "as of first importance." And Paul's addition here about apostolic witness to the risen Jesus was important to the early believers in Jesus for verifying this gospel message. But notice that Paul does not add anything about Jesus being God.

Although I think church creeds can be useful, they always should be subjected to scrutiny. Even the New Testament has some brief credal statements. Many scholars claim 1 Corinthians 15:3–4 is an early, credal and/or confessional formula not original with Paul even though he calls it in other places "my gospel." Yet it was the same gospel the twelve apostles preached (Galatians 2:1-2, 7–9). And for Paul to say, "What I in turn had received," he apparently received it by divine "revelation" rather than "human origin" (Galatians 1:11–12), although scholars debate this.

Also in 1 Corinthians 15:3–4, Paul says twice, "in accordance with the scriptures." What Scriptures? The clause, "That Christ died for our sins," seems to refer to Isaiah 52:13—53:12 and possibly Psalm 22. And Paul saying, "He was raised on the third day," seems to refer to Psalm 16:10. In it, King David addresses God and says, "For you will not abandon my soul to Sheol, or let your holy one see corruption" (ESV).

The Israelites believed that after death, human flesh began to decay on the fourth day. So Psalm 16:10 seems to suggest that a "holy one" will rise from the dead before the fourth day. And on two separate occasions, Peter and Paul preached Jesus's resurrection and supported it by quoting Psalm 16:10 (Acts 2:27–32; 13:34–37). These are examples of Jesus's early disciples deeming it of utmost importance to preach that the Christ event—Jesus's life, death, resurrection, and ascension—fulfilled Bible prophecy.

Paul's Gospel in 2 Corinthians

In 2 Corinthians, Paul defends his apostleship to this church because he founded it, and missionary false apostles were infecting it. Apparently, they were proto-Docetists who preached that Jesus did not possess a physical body, being a phantom, and thus he really didn't suffer a crucifixion death. Paul calls them "false apostles, deceitful workers, disguising themselves as apostles of Christ" (2 Corinthians 11:13).

Also in 2 Corinthians, Paul wrote warning about "another Jesus" and a "different gospel." We considered this in Chapter 2, but it is worthwhile to briefly look at it again. Paul warns those Corinthians, "I am afraid that, as the serpent deceived Eve by its cunning, your thoughts will be led astray from a sincere and pure devotion to Christ. For if someone comes and proclaims another Jesus than the one we proclaimed, or if you receive a different spirit from the one you received, or a different gospel from the one you accepted, you put up with it readily enough" (2 Corinthians 11:3–4). I doubt that Paul would identify the belief that Jesus is God as "another Jesus" because Trinitarians believe strongly in Jesus's atoning death and resurrection. As stated above, Paul likely had in mind incipient Docetism, that Jesus was a phantom who did not suffer death and thus was not raised from the dead.

Paul's Gospel for the Churches of Galatia

Paul wrote to the churches of Galatia to caution them about the Judaizers. He says of these Galatian Christians influenced by them, "You who want to be justified by the law have cut yourselves off from Christ; you have fallen away from grace" (Galatians 5:4). Paul continues, "I am astonished that you are so quickly deserting the one who called you in the grace of Christ and are turning to a different gospel—not that there is another gospel, but there are some who are confusing you and want to pervert the gospel of Christ. But even if we or an angel from heaven should proclaim to you a gospel contrary to what we proclaimed to you, let that one be accursed! As we have said before, so now I repeat, if anyone proclaims to you a gospel contrary to what you received, let that one be accursed!" (Galatians 1:6–9). Wow! Paul again broaches this idea of "a different gospel," just as he had done with the Corinthians. And it is most sobering to ponder him twice denouncing these contrary gospelers as accursed.

Paul began this epistle to the Galatians as he had in most other epistles, "Grace to you and peace from God our Father and the Lord Jesus Christ, who gave himself for our sins ... according to the will of our God and Father" (Galatians 1:3–4). This latter phrase indicates that, for Paul, only the "Father" is "our God." Indeed, Paul later states, "God is one" (3:20). Again, just as Paul wrote in 2 Corinthians 11:4 about "another gospel," one wonders if he would have judged the patristic gospel as "another gospel."

Paul's Gospel in 2 Timothy

Paul wrote to Timothy, his associate in ministry, "Hold to the standard of sound teaching that you have heard from me" (2 Timothy 1:13). Neither Timothy, nor anyone reading this letter, would have been holding to this Pauline standard of teaching if they had added to it that Jesus is God, which Paul never expressly states in any of his letters.

Paul next adds, "Guard the good treasure entrusted to you, with the help of the Holy Spirit living in us" (2 Timothy 1:14). He soon states likewise, "What you have heard from me through many witnesses entrust to faithful people who will be able to teach others as well" (2:2). And Paul adds, "Remember Jesus Christ, raised from the dead, a descendant of David—that is my gospel" (v. 8). So, the apostle Paul's gospel is the Lord Jesus Christ crucified and risen, simple as that!

These admonitions to safeguard Paul's gospel are much like that in the epistle of Jude. Again, it says, "Contend for the faith that was once and for all handed on to the saints" (Jude 4). Surely this and similar texts mean to protect the gospel as Jesus's apostles had intended others to do. Thus, do not tamper with the gospel by adding to it as church fathers later did by saying Jesus is God and that this must be believed to be saved. It must be concluded that they were not being "faithful people" as Paul required.

Paul Was Always a Monotheistic Jew

The apostle Paul was a monotheistic Jew all his life. His New Testament letters reveal that becoming a Christian did not change that. Paul believed there was only one true and living God, whom Jesus called "the/my Father." This is seen especially in all the salutations in Paul's letters. In them, he distinguishes between God the Father and Jesus Christ as two separate persons, and Paul never expressly identifies Jesus as "God."

Moreover, Paul often relates that Jesus had a God as the following reveal:

- "The God and Father of our Lord Jesus Christ" (Romans 15:6; 2 Corinthians 1:3; Ephesians 1:3)
- "The God and Father of the Lord Jesus" (2 Corinthians 11:31)
- "the God of our Lord Jesus Christ, the Father of glory" (Ephesians 1:17)
- "God, the Father of our Lord Jesus Christ" (Colossians 1:3)

In Paul's first New Testament epistle he writes, "Grace be to you and peace from God our Father and the Lord Jesus Christ. First, I thank my God through Jesus Christ for all of you" (Romans 1:7–8). He soon declares that "God is one" (3:30). Paul concludes this epistle by giving tribute to "the eternal God ... the only wise God, through Jesus Christ" (16:26–27). Paul often says access to God the Father occurs exclusively "through Jesus Christ." Jesus himself once made this exclusivity clear by declaring, "I am the way, and the truth, and the life. No one comes to the Father except through me" (John 14:6).

Trinitarians claim they are monotheistic. Yet many people conclude they worship three Gods. In contrast, Paul's strict monotheism emerges as he writes, "There is no God but one. ... there is one God, the Father ... and one Lord Jesus Christ" (1 Corinthians 8:4, 6). Paul likewise writes elsewhere about "one Lord, one faith, one baptism, one God and Father of all" (Ephesians 4:6). Paul's literary habit was to identify exclusively Jesus as "Lord" and "the Father" as "God." Thus, the apostle Paul was always, as we might say, "a good Jew" by keeping the Shema, which says God is "one" (Deuteronomy 6:4).

The apostle Paul demonstrates his monotheism so majestically when he writes to his apostolic associate Timothy about God the Father by declaring, "To the King of the ages, immortal, invisible, the only God, be honor and glory forever and ever. Amen" (1 Timothy 1:17). He follows this by saying of "God our Savior" that he "is one God" and "there is one mediator between God and humankind, Christ Jesus, himself human, who gave himself a ransom for all" (2:5–6). Here, Paul distinguishes between the Father as God and Jesus as human. This text does not mean Jesus is a God-man as Trinitarians often assert. Paul ends this epistle, saying of God, "he who is the blessed and only Sovereign, the King of kings and Lord of lords. It is he alone who has immortality and dwells in unapproachable light, whom no one has ever seen or can see" (6:15–16).

Grammatical Difficulties in Some Pauline Texts

The ancient New Testament manuscripts that textual critics use to compile a text from which versions are translated were hand-copied by scribes using the Koine Greek language. Recall that ancient languages were not as sophisticated as ours are nowadays. These Koine Greek manuscripts were written in uncials, which do not have lowercase, spaces between words, or even any punctuation at all. So, grammatical difficulties arise more often in them than in modern-language documents. Plus, linguists sometimes disagree whether some grammatical rule existed then.

We have learned that the consensus of distinguished scholars who have written books about whether the New Testament identifies Jesus as God have cited about nine "major" texts having the word *God* (Gr.

theos) that traditionalists have cited to support their view that Jesus is God. These are John 1:1, 18; 20:28; Romans 9:5; 2 Thessalonians 1:12; Titus 2:13; Hebrews 1:.8; 2 Peter 1:.1; 1 John 5:20. Notice that three of them are in Paul's letters. A grammatical difficulty occurs in all three of them, and it causes English versions to differ on how to translate them. For instance, some versions translate the end of Romans 9:5 as saying "Christ/Messiah" is "God over all, blessed forever" or the like, thereby identifying Christ as "God," yet other versions render it "Christ/Messiah. God, who is over all, be blessed forever" or the like, which does not call Christ "God."

A syntax (word order) problem occurs in 2 Thessalonians 1:12, Titus 2:13, and 2 Peter 1:1. Consequently, some English versions translate these texts by applying "God" (Gr. *theos*) to Jesus, thereby calling him "God," yet other versions have "God" referring to the Father so that these texts do not call Jesus "God." I believe that to decide what the author meant in cases that have grammatical difficulties, it is best to allot considerable credence to the whole document and in Paul's case also his entire biblical corpus. Thus, since Paul nowhere expressly identifies Jesus as God in his entire corpus, he most likely did not intend to do so in these cases with grammatical difficulties.

Distinguished scholars generally have agreed that the New Testament contains three foremost texts that generally have been understood as identifying Jesus as God: John 1:1c; 20:28; Philippians 2:5–11. So the latter is Pauline. I believe the "human interpretation" of Philippians 2:6–7, which is strongly advocated and articulated by Trinitarian James D. G. Dunn, known for his expertise on Christology, is correct, and it does not identify Jesus as God. Now, I have examined these three texts extensively in *The Restitution* and cited many eminent New Testament scholars in doing so.[39]

Conclusion

We have seen that the apostle Paul is very clear in his New Testament letters in saying that Jesus's atoning death and resurrection are central to his gospel and thus necessary to believe to receive divine forgiveness, salvation, and eternal life. And Paul often explains that making Jesus Lord is the necessary outcome of true, saving faith.

When church fathers of the fourth and fifth centuries added to the gospel that Jesus is God, and made this a necessary faith requirement

---

[39] John 1:1c (13 pp.); John 20:28 (17 pp.); Philippians 2:5–11 (21 pp.).

for salvation, they came close to declaring "another Jesus" and creating "a different gospel" than what Paul preached. For, when Paul writes of the gospel in his corpus, he never says explicitly Jesus is God.

To the Corinthians, we have seen that Paul likely had in mind proto-Docetists who claimed Jesus did not have a fleshly body and therefore did not suffer on the cross. And to the Galatians, Paul was thinking of Judaizers who called for a return to ritual that cannot save. These false teachings resulted in "another Jesus" and "a different gospel" that were worse than what church fathers did in adding to Paul's gospel that Jesus was God. However, it cannot be denied that they changed Paul's gospel without his authorization and that it therefore needs to be restored.

I conclude this chapter with these excerpts from *The Restitution* (pp. 395–396):

> Seventeen years are Paul's conversion this successful yet humble and determined servant of God traveled to Jerusalem to procure the apostles' scrutiny of his gospel message. Paul writes, "I submitted to them the gospel which I preach among the Gentiles" (Gal 2:2). Paul relates that their judgment was that his gospel was substantially the same as their own (Gal 2:7–10; cf. Acts 15).
>
> We have seen that many traditionalists now concede to the critics' allegation that traditional Christology represents a substantial change from the primitive Christology. But they usually insist that the church was divinely authorized to do so. If true, then why did the Apostle Paul feel compelled to submit his gospel to his predecessors for their approval? Was it not because Paul wanted to be sure that he had not changed the original gospel about Jesus Christ, the gospel that was handed down by Jesus's twelve apostles? ...
>
> *Paul absolutely forbade altering the gospel he preached and passed on to others.* Neither did he tolerate theological speculation of his gospel and Jesus's identity. Paul wrote about his missionary teams: "We are destroying speculations and every lofty thing raised up against the knowledge of God" (2 Cor 10:5).
>
> These excerpts from Paul's letters suggest that he would have disagreed with later church fathers in their development of Christology by changing the primitive gospel of Jesus as no more than a man to His being God. *The original gospel of Jesus Christ did not need to be developed; it already was. Paul merely expected his successors to receive and preach it as he had, not to change it.*

Chapter 8
Relations Between Three Monotheistic Religions

Church fathers put an unnecessary obstacle in the path of many truth seekers by requiring that they believe in the incarnation to be saved. Again, classic "incarnation" means Jesus preexisted as God and came down from heaven to become a man, resulting in him being a God-man. Incarnation is a stumbling block to people who well reason that it is impossible for God to become a man. Plus, it is an unnecessary hindrance to dialogue especially between the three monotheistic religions of the world, which is a lot of people. It is important for religions to be in dialogue with one another. How religions get along with one another can have a huge impact on world peace.

What the Three Monotheistic Religions Believe about God

The three main monotheistic religions in the world are Judaism, Christianity, and Islam.[40] There are just over 8 billion people in the world. One third of them, about 2.6 billion people, profess to be Christian; one fourth of them, about 2 billion people, claim to be Muslim; and a small fraction of them are religious Jews, from whose roots came these other two largest religions in the world for many centuries. So, monotheistic worshippers of the same (?) deity consist of well over half of the world's population. How have these three monotheistic religions related in the identification of their God?

The bedrock of the Jewish religion has always been the Shema in the Torah. It states, "Hear, O Israel: The LORD our God, the LORD is one" (Deuteronomy 6:4 ESV). Jews have believed the Hebrew word used here, *echad*, means numerically "one" just as it does elsewhere. This text, therefore, has been the main basis for Jewish monotheism.

---
[40] Technically, identifying those religions in antiquity as "monotheist" is anachronistic. I mean their adherents worshipped only one God, usually denying the existence of other Gods.

Islam strongly agrees with Judaism that there is only one God who created the universe. Islam affirms this constantly in its sacred text, the Qur'an.

As for Christianity, historians recognize it as a monotheistic religion with a caveat that its adherents worship three Persons, each designated as God in a single Godhead. Ever since the close of the fourth century, the Christian religion has been Trinitarian. This means that God is three Persons: Father, Son (Jesus Christ), and Holy Spirit. Until recently, Trinitarian scholars asserted Jesus is not only God but "God the Son," "the Second Person of the Trinity." All of this clashes with both Judaism and Islam. Both regard Christianity as polytheistic—the worship of multiple Gods. This disagreement about theology makes dialogue of Christians with Jews and Muslims more difficult.

How did this dispute between these three monotheistic religions occur?

Early Jewish Christians and Judaism

Scholars distinguish between "the Jesus Movement," which consisted mostly of early Jewish believers in Jesus, and "Christianity," which succeeded it and consisted increasingly of Gentile believers in Jesus due to the spreading of the gospel worldwide. The early Jesus movement is called "the Way" in the book of Acts.[41] "Jewish Christians" existed mostly as a distinct group separate from Christianity.[42] They existed as two sects: larger Ebionites and Nazarenes. The latter traced their heritage to Acts 24:5. It says Paul was accused of being "a ringleader of the sect of the Nazarenes." Both sects believed in Jesus's atoning death and resurrection while adhering to the Law of Moses and rejecting Paul's letters. Nazarenes believed in Jesus's virgin birth, but some Ebionites did not. Both Ebionites and Nazarenes believed Jesus was no more than a man, thus not God. This denial brought these Jewish Christians increasingly into conflict with Catholic Christianity until they disappeared or were absorbed by the Catholic Church in the fifth century.

Those Jewish Christians had been ostracized by both synagogue and church. At first, they attended synagogue to stay faithful to their religious heritage. But increasing conflict ensued between them and

---

[41] Acts 9:2; 19:9, 23; 22:4; 24:14, 22; cf. John 14:6.
[42] The designation "Jewish Christian" is still much debated by scholars as to its legitimacy.

Rabbinic Judaism until the latter identified them as *minim*, meaning "heretics," for believing in Jesus and expelled them from the synagogue. The Catholic Church rejected them primarily because they denied Jesus was God. In such disagreements, where there are two sides with some people in the middle, the middle group often are more correct about the matter. That is how I believe this disagreement was between Christianity and Judaism—the Jewish Christians in the middle, who were called Nazarenes, were nearest the truth.

The Parting of the Ways

Catholic Christianity and Rabbinic Judaism became increasingly hostile toward each other until there was what scholars call "the parting of the ways." It was a gradual process that occurred between the Jews' First Jewish Revolt against Rome in 66–70 CE and the Second Jewish Revolt against Rome in 132–135 CE. After the destruction of the temple at Jerusalem in 70 CE, Pharisees developed Rabbinic Judaism as a replacement for Second Temple Judaism. The Catholic Church cited the temple's destruction as proof that God had abandoned Jews because they rejected Jesus as the Messiah. The Church became increasingly antisemitic, alleging that God had transferred to the Church all Bible promises to Jews. This is now called "supersessionism" or "replacement theory."

Yet, the main plank that divided Rabbinic Judaism and Catholic Christianity was the Church's identification of Jesus as God. Jacob Neusner—a Jewish, Bible scholar and prolific author I once met[43]—explains, "A review of the medieval disputations will turn up ample evidence that the Judaic party regarded the claim of incarnation as decisive proof of Christianity's implausibility—indeed, incomprehensibility. So it must follow that the parties parted company at incarnation .... [that] Jesus is God incarnate."[44]

I suspect if church fathers had not been so antisemitic during the early centuries of Christianity—dismissing God's plan for his chosen people and their nation—they may have listened to Jews about their contention that *God is one* and not fallen into the error

---

[43] Dr. Scot McKnight introduced me to Dr. Jacob Neusner. Scot inquired, "Jacob, how many books have you written?" He answered, "Six hundred." Scot, a prolific author himself, asked again, "How can *anyone* write six hundred books?" Professor Neusner replied matter-of-factly, "Oh, it wasn't that hard."

[44] Jacob Neusner and Bruce Chilton, *Jewish-Christian Debates: God, Kingdom, Messiah* (Minneapolis: Fortress, 1998), 217.

of proclaiming an incarnation and God being three Persons. Philip Alexander explains:

> Traditionally Christianity has defined itself in opposition to Judaism: a central element of its self-assertion had been that it is *not* Judaism. Two events of the twentieth century have, indeed, strongly challenged this traditional Christian position. The Holocaust has called into question Christian anti-Judaism. And the renaissance of Judaism in modern times, with the establishment of the State of Israel, has cast doubt on Christian triumphalist assumptions that Jews are politically powerless, their culture a fossilized anachronism.[45]

Muslims and their Qur'an

Muhammad founded the religion of Islam in the year 610 CE while experiencing visions in a cave. The Arabic word *islam* means "submission." Believers of Islam are called Muslims, meaning "to surrender." Islam is based on a religious text called "the Qur'an." Muslims believe Muhammad uttered sayings that became the Qur'an. Muslims are encouraged to memorize the Qur'an to strengthen them in their religious faith.

Muhammad was a caravan trader who was exposed to various religious beliefs, especially those of Jews and Christians. Thus, the Qur'an is strongly monotheistic. It calls God "Allah" since that is the Arabic word for "God." The Qur'an affirms the Jewish Bible as "the word of God;" yet Muslims believe it was corrupted in its transmission.

The Qur'an contains many statements relating to Judaism and Christianity. It often affirms the future resurrection and the judgment. It says Jesus was "the Messiah" (5:72, 75), he had a virgin birth (19:20–21), and he ascended to heaven (3:57). One Qur'an text seems Docetic by denying Jesus was crucified, died, and arose from the dead (4:157). The Qur'an denies Jesus was God (5:16, 72, 116; 9:30–31), rejects the doctrine of the Trinity (4:71–72; 5:73), and affirms many times that God is numerically "one." For instance, it hints at Christians deifying Jesus by saying to Jews, "People of the Book, let us come to an agreement that we will worship none but God, that we will associate none with Him, and that none of us will set up mortals as deities besides God" (3:63).

---

[45] Philip S. Alexander, "'The Parting of the Ways' from the Perspective of Rabbinic Judaism," in James D. G. Dunn, ed., *Jews and Christians: The Parting of the Ways, A.D. 70 to 135* (orig. 1992; Grand Rapids: Eerdmans, 1999), 1.

Are Trinitarians Monotheists or Polytheists?

So, are Trinitarians polytheists for worshipping three Gods, as Jews and Muslims assert? If so, should they be regarded as pseudo-Christians? It is questionable that Trinitarians worship three Gods. I think it *looks* that way. Trinitarians saying 1=3 is not only terrible math but irrational thinking. Nevertheless, they adamantly deny they worship three Gods. Even if they do, we have as a possible guide a precedent for this in Scripture that suggests Trinitarians ought not be rendered as non-Christian polytheists.

There is a saying in sports, perhaps more so in golf, "It's not how you start but how you finish." Yeah, it often *seems* that way. Yet, the first stroke in golf counts the same on the scorecard as the last stroke does. Plus, this saying appears biblical. Wise King Solomon wrote, "Better is the end of a thing than its beginning" (Ecclesiastes 7:8).

That precedent is King Solomon himself. His father, David, wanted to build a temple for God. But God told David through the prophet Nathan, "When your days are fulfilled and you lie down with your ancestors, I will raise up your offspring after you, who shall come forth from your body, and I will establish his kingdom. He shall build a house for my name, and I will establish the throne of his kingdom forever. I will be a father to him, and he shall be a son to me. When he commits iniquity, I will punish him with a rod such as mortals use, with blows inflicted by human beings. But I will not take my steadfast love from him" (2 Samuel 7:12–15). God was talking about King Solomon.

God did not quit loving King Solomon as his own even though the king started great and finished rather miserably by worshipping other gods along with Yahweh, the God of Israel. We read, "King Solomon loved many foreign women. ... Among his wives were seven hundred princesses and three hundred concubines; and his wives turned away his heart. For when Solomon was old, his wives turned away his heart after other gods, and his heart was not true to the LORD his God, as was the heart of his father David" (1 Kings 11:1, 3–4). So, because of this, God brought trouble upon Solomon. Yet the text says, "his God," signifying that Solomon remained God's "son" just as God had promised through Nathan, "I will be a father to him, and he shall be a son to me."

I think in considering this case about Solomon, Trinitarians should be accepted as Christians even though it appears to some people that they worship three Gods. I would just say, "Trinis are mixed up." And I've already related in Chapter 1 how I was a Christian believer even though I was a Trinitarian for twenty-two years.

I address this in the preface in *The Restitution* (p. xx) as follows:

In 1999, a doctrinal declaration was issued and signed by over a hundred evangelical Christian leaders, mostly Americans, which includes the following article: "We deny that any view of Jesus Christ which reduces or rejects his full deity is Gospel faith or will avail to salvation." I could react as contrarily by charging that anyone who believes in the doctrine of Trinity worships three gods and thereby violates the First Commandment, as Sir Isaac Newton alleged and the Koran states (Quran 5:72–73), and thus cannot be a true Christian. But I reject such allegations.

Conclusion

The British scholars who contributed to *The Myth of God Incarnate* (1977) book were right in so titling it.[46] Its back cover says it was "the most talked about religious book" of its day. Francis Young well explains in it, "The notion of God being incarnate in the traditionally accepted sense is read into, not out of, the Pauline epistles ... the same could be argued for the other New Testament documents." The preface of this book also says, "Christianity can only remain honestly believable by being continuously open to the truth."[47] Amen! And doing so will surely improve any dialogue between these three main monotheistic religions in the world. It may even contribute to Jesus's beatitude, "Blessed are the peacemakers, for they will be called children of God" (Matthew 5:9).

---

[46] John Hick, ed., *The Myth of God Incarnate* (London: SCM/Philadelphia: Westminster, 1977).
[47] Hick, *The Myth of God Incarnate*, 22, x.

Chapter 9
Did the Gospel Evolve and Did Jesus Know Who He Was?

Clearly, church fathers changed the gospel. Church historian and Trinitarian R. P. C. Hanson acknowledges this in his massive and unrivaled examination of the Arian Controversy. He relates, "There is no doubt, however, that the pro-Nicene theologians throughout the controversy were engaged in a process of developing doctrine and consequently introducing what must be called a change in doctrine. ... I believe that it was necessary and right ... that it was a change can hardly be denied."[48] Yes, but was it "necessary and right"? Was this patristic change of the primitive gospel authorized by God? If it was changed, God must approve it or else it is a forgery and thus a corruption.

We have seen that Jude seems to implicitly warn against changing the gospel by exhorting, "Contend for the faith that was once for all entrusted to the saints" (Jude 3). So be faithful to the original gospel that Jesus's early disciples preached and passed on to others. *Don't change the gospel*! And we saw in Chapter 7 that Paul went to Jerusalem to ask the apostles there if his gospel was the same as theirs. They said it was, and none of them said Jesus was God. Paul would not have done that if he had thought the primitive gospel given to him needed to be developed in the sense of changing it.

What Twentieth-Century Bible Scholars Said about Jesus's Identity

During the nineteenth century, German liberal scholars were the first to establish persuasively that church fathers changed the original gospel. Nobel Peace Prize recipient Albert Schweitzer and church historian Adolf von Harnack did this in their very highly acclaimed books.[49] They excelled at separating Christian origins from patristic church dogma. Harnack demolished Nicene-Chalcedonian Christology, especially its hypostatic union of Christ. In *What Is Christianity?*,

---
[48] Hanson, *The Search for the Christian Doctrine of God*, 872–73.
[49] Albert Schweitzer, *The Quest of the Historical Jesus* (1906); Adolf von Harnack, *The History of Dogma*, 7 vols. (1894–1899).

Harnack quotes 1 Corinthians 15:3–4 and says, "Paul did, it is true, make Christ's death and resurrection ... the whole of the gospel."[50]

Conservative, traditionalist scholars in the latter half of the twentieth century differed. Oscar Cullmann, Ferdinand Hahn, C. F. D. Moule, and Raymond E. Brown agreed with liberal scholars by saying the early New Testament documents—such as the Synoptic Gospels and perhaps Paul's letters—do not identify Jesus as God, but the later Gospel of John does. However, they disagreed with them by asserting that a "development" in the New Testament from Jesus as a man to a God-man was correct. Liberal scholars said it was not and therefore dismissed the Gospel of John as being historically inauthentic.

Many of these conservative scholars based this christological "development" on their dating of the New Testament documents. They reasoned that its early writings do not call Jesus "God" whereas its later writings do, thus allowing time for this supposed christological development. That is why we learned in Chapter 4 about Raymond E. Brown claiming the only New Testament texts that identify Jesus as "God" are in the later writings, such as John 1:1, 20:28, and Hebrews 1:8. He says, "The sermons which Acts attributes to the beginning of the Christian mission do not speak of Jesus as God. Thus, there is no reason to think that Jesus was called God in the earliest layers of New Testament tradition. ... The New Testament does call Jesus 'God,' but this is a development of the later New Testament books."[51]

All scholars call this early Christology in the Synoptics a "low Christology" since it has Jesus only as a man. They say the later Gospel of John has a "high Christology" since they believe it depicts Jesus as a God-man. Liberal scholars also argued that this change from a low to a high Christology was "evolutionary." They were correct in asserting that *Jesus never said he was God*. They also concluded that *Jesus didn't believe he was God*.

Brown strangely objects to asking this question. He writes, "Often theologians prefer to study the problem of Jesus's knowledge of his divinity in terms of the question: 'Did Jesus know he was God?' From a biblical viewpoint this question is so badly phrased that it cannot be answered and should not be posed."[52] What! Brown provides

---

[50] Adolf von Harnack, *What Is Christianity?* tr. T. B. Saunders (orig. 1900; New York: Harper, 1957), 153-54.

[51] Brown, *Jesus God and Man: Modern Biblical Reflections* (New York: MacMillan, 1967), 30, 86.

[52] Brown, *Jesus God and Man*, 86.

no rationale for this surprising assessment in 1967, when this book was published.

Moule argued against an "evolutionary" process that alleges that there was a departure from the original gospel. He favors the "developmental" process. He explains, "The change from (say) invoking Jesus as a revered Master" in the Synoptic Gospels "to the acclamation of him as a divine Lord" in John's gospel "only attempts to describe what was already there from the beginning."[53] So, Moule claimed a smooth continuance between Jesus's self-consciousness as God and later church fathers saying he was God.

Moule was James (Jimmy) D. G. Dunn's PhD dissertation supervisor. Dunn's book *The Making of Christology* (1980) made him the preeminent authority on New Testament Christology for decades. I met the cordial Jimmy Dunn in 2000 when he was the guest speaker of the first annual, Zarley Lectures at North Park University. (I was the initial donor of these lectures.) That weekend, I was honored to room together with Dr. Dunn and Dr. Scot McKnight (founder and director of these lectures) at the annual meeting of the Society of Biblical Literature (SBL). That is when I asked Jimmy if he was sure the Bible says Jesus is God. He said there is only one text that made him certain: John 1:1c ("and the Word was God") compared with v. 14 ("the Word became flesh"). At that time, Dunn followed Moule in accepting the developmental hypothesis.[54]

I believe this high Christology view of mostly the Gospel of John, held by liberal and conservative scholars alike, is incorrect. Like the Synoptics, the Fourth Gospel does *not* say Jesus is God. In this, I am aligned with Johannine scholar John A. T. Robinson in his book *The Priority of John*. Robinson and C. H. Dodd were perhaps the foremost British Bible scholars in the twentieth century. Robinson believed high Christology does not appear in the New Testament and that it first developed following the first century, mostly with the Nicene Council in 325. In the second and third centuries church fathers, called "apologists," had believed Jesus was divine but to a lesser extent than the Father was. They thereby rightly regarded the Father as the

---

[53] C.F.D. Moule, *The Origin of Christology* (Cambridge: University, 1977), 1–3.
[54] I have been an SBL member since 1999 and have attended every annual meeting since then except one. In the preface of Dunn's book, *A New Perspective on Jesus* (p. 7), he mentions the "Zarley Lectures, North Park University, Chicago (2000)" along with other lectures he did during that time and explains, "These lectures all led up to the publication of my large-scale work *Jesus Remembered* (2003)."

Almighty who was supreme overall, thus including over Jesus. I explain this in *The Restitution* (p. 64) as follows:

> Traditionalists have defended this development by insisting that later church fathers needed time to reflect upon the meaning of the Christ-event and that their explanations (some would call them "additions") of the gospel were biblically accurate. Some traditionalists have contended that the theological positions that emerged victorious from controversy did so as evidence of their veracity as well as God's sovereignty.
>
> On the contrary, F. Young gets it right by alleging, "There are strong reasons then for seeing the patristic development and interpretation of incarnational belief, not as a gradual dawning of the truth inspired by the Holy Spirit, but as a historically determined development which led to the blind alleys of paradox, illogicality and Docetism."[55]

The Lausanne Movement

And what was happening outside the halls of the academia during this time? Well, The International Congress on World Evangelism was held in 1974 in Lausanne, Switzerland. It lasted ten days and was led by Evangelist Billy Graham. More than 2,300 evangelical leaders from more than 150 nations attended. Its stated purpose was "to define the necessity, responsibilities, and goals of spreading the Gospel." Its primary outcome was the creation of The Lausanne Covenant, a fifteen-point Statement of Faith. Hundreds of para-church groups, especially missionary organizations, have used it. They have viewed it as one of the most important documents in modern church history.

The Covenant begins, "We affirm our belief in the one eternal God, Creator and Lord of the world, Father, Son and Holy Spirit, who governs all things according to the purpose of his will." This unwittingly affirms modalism of Oneness Pentecostals—that God is one Person existing as three modes—more than it does Trinitarianism. And it adds that Jesus Christ is "the only God-man." The gospel is later defined correctly as "the good news that Jesus Christ died for our sins and was raised from the dead according to the Scriptures." It also reads, "We need both watchfulness and discernment to safeguard the biblical gospel." Indeed. Overall, I think The Lausanne Covenant is a pretty good statement that

---

[55] F. Young, "A Cloud of Witnesses," ed. John Hick, *The Myth of God Incarnate* (Philadelphia: Westminster, 1977), 29.

could be improved concerning the "one God." However, saying Jesus is a "God-man," which the Bible never says, should be deleted.

Follow-up Lausanne conferences were held in 1989 and 2010.

The Evangelical Quadrilateral

Evangelicalism is a continuing movement that first emerged in Germany and then took root in the eighteenth century in Great Britain and America as a revival of Protestantism. Its emphasis has been on being Bible-centered, which contrasts with credal-centered, and on spreading the gospel worldwide. *If a person is an evangelical, she or he is certainly a Christian since an evangelical is a certain type of Christian.*

It has never been easy to define evangelicalism. One effort at doing so has been the Evangelical Quadrilateral. This definition has been adopted by several Christian organizations, including the National Association of Evangelicals (NAE) in the US. It was drafted in 1988 by church history professor David Bebbington of Scotland. He is an authority on the history of evangelicalism. Also called "the Bebbington Quadrilateral," it has four points: Bible authority, Jesus's crucifixion, conversion, and social justice. It says evangelicals stress the necessity of believing in Jesus's atoning death for our sins and his resurrection from the dead. But it contains nothing about the "deity of Christ" (=Jesus is God) or God as three Persons, yet the NAE includes these in its Statement of Faith. So, I would like to know why the Bebbington Quadrilateral does not include the requirement to believe in the deity of Christ and God as three Persons. Does Bebbington and the NAE believe people are evangelicals, thus Christians, if they believe all four points of the Quadrilateral even if they deny the deity of Christ and the Trinity doctrine?

More recently, the NAE joined LifeWay Research in a research project involving numerous theologians and social scientists to further define evangelicalism. Their result is that an evangelical is a person who believes (1) the Bible is the ultimate authority for faith, (2) personal evangelism is important, (3) Jesus's death atoned for our sins, and (4) only Jesus as Savior provides eternal salvation. Like the Quadrilateral, neither does this definition mention the deity of Christ or God being three Persons.

Thus, *according to these two definitions I am an evangelical and therefore a Christian*. And the NAE seems to disagree with most church fathers who said otherwise.

There are many professing Christians, some like me, who strongly believe all these points, yet we do not believe in the deity of Christ or the doctrine of the Trinity. Oneness Pentecostals and Christadelphians are well known for believing this way. And there are some Church of God denominations that believe likewise. So I think there needs to be a public discussion on whether a person can believe in all these above points and not believe in the deity of Christ and the Trinity doctrine yet be an evangelical—but more importantly, be a genuine Christian.

Frankly, I don't care much about being labeled evangelical. But *I care a lot about being known as a Christian.* I'll share a personal story. I was in the US Army Reserves for seven years. One year, I was processing into a two-week summer camp at the Yakima Firing Range in my home state of Washington. A sergeant looked at my paperwork and said, "Zarley, what's your religion?" I answered, "Christian, sir." He replied tersely, "Zarley, you *can't* be a Christian. You gotta be a Baptist, a Catholic, a Methodist, a Presbyterian, or something like that." I said modestly, "Sir, I'm none of those things. I'm a Christian." He looked up at me from his chair with an irritated look on his face, shook his head, and moved on. I think he thought, "I can't help this hardheaded private."

"The Gospel of Jesus Christ: An Evangelical Celebration"

In *The Restitution* (p. 113), I relate that as the twentieth century was ending:

> In 1999, a group of fifteen Evangelical leaders drafted an extensive doctrinal statement of approximately ten pages in length that purportedly defines the NT gospel. It is entitled, "The Gospel of Jesus Christ: An Evangelical Celebration." This drafting committee included leading Evangelical scholars J. I. Packer, D. A. Carson, R. C. Sproul, and John Woodbridge. Over 200 Evangelical leaders and scholars signed this declaration. The list of signatories includes such illustrious men of God as Billy Graham, Bill Bright, Jerry Falwell, Pat Robertson, Charles Colson, John Stott, Charles Swindoll, John Walvoord, and many other well-known names.[56] Their statement describes Jesus Christ as "God

---

[56] John N. Akers, John H. Armstrong, and John D. Woodbridge, eds., *This We Believe: The Good News of Jesus Christ for the World* (Grand Rapids: Zondervan, 2000), 18, 249–52.

the Son, the second Person of the Holy Trinity." It continues, "We affirm that faith in Jesus Christ as the divine Word (or Logos, John 1:1), the second Person of the Trinity, co-eternal and co-essential with the Father and the Holy Spirit (Heb. 1:3), is foundational to faith in the Gospel. We deny that any view of Jesus Christ which reduces or rejects his full deity is Gospel faith or will avail to salvation. We affirm that Jesus Christ is God incarnate (John 1:14)."[57] The drafters claim that their statement reflects the major creeds of Christianity. Indeed. But do these excerpts from it reflect the Bible?

In this statement of faith, this evangelical group further relates, "This Gospel is the only Gospel: there is no other; and to change its substance is to pervert and indeed destroy it." No, *you* have changed the substance of the original gospel, but I wouldn't say you've destroyed it. People are saved if they believe what your gospel says: Jesus died for our sins and rose from the dead. Adding that he "is God" is a corruption.

As we have seen, not only does the Bible not contain the language "God the Son," "Trinity," or "second Person of the Trinity," even the concepts indicated by this language do not appear in the New Testament in any of its sermons or descriptions of the gospel (Gr. *euangelion*). How could so many evangelical leaders be so misguided when their moniker "evangelical" derives from the Greek word *euangelion*? While evangelicals have claimed to adhere faithfully to the gospel and make the Bible the basis of their faith, they often have allowed church creeds to dominate them. In fact, their statement claims to reflect "The Patristic Rule of Faith, the historic creeds, the Reformation confessions." But you can't have it both ways. It's either the Bible's primitive gospel or church creeds.

Did Dunn Continue to Believe Jesus Was God?

Since James D. G. Dunn was regarded by many as the foremost authority on New Testament Christology, it is worth examining briefly one of his later books entitled *Did the First Christians Worship Jesus?*[58] His answer to this question is a resounding "no." Thus, he seems to have altered his view about Jesus's identity, as if he no longer believed Jesus is God as he did in *Christology in the Making*. Yet, he does not

---

[57] Quoted from *This We Believe*, 239, 245. Also see it in *Christianity Today*, June 1999.
[58] James D. G. Dunn, *Did the First Christians Worship Jesus? The New Testament Evidence* (London: SPCK/Louisville: WJK, 2010).

admit to a changed viewpoint. He may have continued embracing the developmental hypothesis, whether he believed it occurred in John's Gospel or, later, in the patristic era. I will now arrange citations from this book in bulleted form without making any comments:

- "Was Jesus a monotheist? ... Yes. Jesus was a monotheist; he confessed God as one. ... He worshipped God alone" (p. 101).
- "Jesus was God, in that he made God known. ... He was not God in himself" (p. 135).
- "John had no qualms in depicting Jesus as defending himself against the charge that he was making himself God by citing the fact that Ps. 82:6 called other human beings 'gods' (John 10:33–35)" (p. 135).
- "Jesus is not the God of Israel. He is not the Father. He is not Yahweh" (p. 142).
- "Jesus ... was not to be worshipped as wholly God, or fully identified with God, far less as a god. If he was worshipped it was worship offered to God in and through him. ... Only God, only the one God, is to be worshipped" (p. 146).
- "Christian worship can deteriorate into what may be called Jesus-olatry. ... The danger of Jesus-olatry is ... that Jesus has been substituted for God, has taken the place of the one creator God; Jesus is absorbing the worship due to God alone. ... The worship due to God is stopping at Jesus. ... The revelation of God through Jesus and the worship of God through Jesus is being stifled and short-circuited" (p. 147).
- "Did the first Christians worship Jesus? ... No, by and large the first Christians did not worship Jesus as such. ... Christianity remains a monotheistic faith. The only one to be worshipped is the one God" (pp. 150–51).

For Dunn to say, "Jesus was God, in that he made God known. ... He was not God in himself," I think that is a clear statement of a God-in-Christ Christology as opposed to a Christ-is-God Christology, which is what this book and *The Restitution* are all about.

Wright and Hurtado Say Jesus Didn't Know Who He Was

I related in Chapter 1 that when I had that moment of enlightenment that led to my research into Jesus's identity, I asked myself how I should begin such a study. And I answered, "No one knows better who Jesus was than Jesus did." Well, some of the leading Trinitarian scholars in the world, and close friends of Jimmy Dunn, now surprisingly disagree with that—that Jesus knew who he was! No joke!

Returning to the academic pursuit called "the quest for the historical Jesus," by the turn of the century members of the Jesus Seminar had argued most compellingly that Jesus never claimed he was God and never thought he was God. Because of this advance, or correction, in Christian theology, Trinitarian scholars such as N. T. (Tom) Wright and Larry Hurtado shifted to embrace this viewpoint while also adopting the strange notion that *even though Jesus did not believe he was God, he really was*!

Tom Wright is regarded by many of his peers and book publishers as the world's foremost New Testament scholar and Jesus researcher. He used to be a bishop in the Anglican Church and a chaplain to Queen Elizabeth. I know this charming, witty, and erudite fellow with the thick British accent. I once had dinner with him and his wife, Maggie. Tom believes Jesus was and is God. But in his books Tom sometimes does some fancy dancing around this issue.[59] In three of his books, he halts this delicate tip-toeing, adopts a firm stance, and declares boldly, "I do not think Jesus 'knew he was God.'"[60] His friend Larry Hurtado joined the dance music by agreeing most heartily.

Hurtado followed Martin Hengel's little book, *The Son of God*, by championing the viewpoint that the first Christians worshipped Jesus as "divine." Hurtado claimed most assuredly that it was "easily within the first decade of the Christian movement."[61] But, again, historical Jesus researchers argued that the early disciples of Jesus, having been monotheistic Jews, could not have changed that soon to believing that both the Father and Jesus were God, which many Jesus researchers regarded as two Gods.

I also knew Larry Hurtado. He was the guest lecturer at the Zarley Lectures in 2008. About ten years later, I heard Larry speak at an SBL annual meeting forum attended by over one hundred scholars. The shift

---

[59] E.g., N. T. Wright, *Who Was Jesus?* (London: SPCK/Grand Rapids: Eerdmans, 1992), 51.

[60] N. T. Wright, *The Challenge of Jesus: Rediscovering Who Jesus Was and Is* (Downers Grove, IL: IVP, 1999), 121; Marcus J. Borg and N. T. Wright, *The Meaning of Jesus: Two Visions* (New York: HarperCollins, 1999), 166; cf. N. T. Wright, *Jesus and the Victory of God* (Minneapolis: Fortress, 1996), 653.

[61] Larry W. Hurtado, *One God, One Lord: Early Christian Devotion and Ancient Jewish Monotheism* (London: SCM, 1988), 5.

was occurring in the academy, even among some evangelicals, to this view that Jesus did not believe he was God. So, in the Q&A, someone asked Larry if Jesus believed he was God. Larry answered startlingly, "*Hell* no!" Yet, like Tom Wright, Larry Hurtado still believed Jesus was and is God.

If Jesus didn't know he was God, then he didn't believe he was God. And if Jesus didn't believe he was God, why should *we* believe he was God? Moreover, if Jesus didn't believe he was God, how can our salvation depend on us believing he was God, as Trinis claim? Now that's a brain twister I'd like Dr. N. T. Wright the Trinitarian to answer!

It seems ludicrous to me that these very intelligent and scholarly gentlemen could believe Jesus did not know or believe he was God, yet they themselves believed he was. So, *Wright and Hurtado claimed to know better who Jesus was than Jesus did!* I don't see how those guys avoided getting laughed out of town for that! It shows the ridiculous lengths to which people can go in hanging on to belief that Jesus is God. It reminds me of what I wrote in *The Restitution* (p. 72) about Thomas Aquinas's belief in the beatific vision. It forced him to declare most absurdly of Jesus, "He could not have had faith."

Conclusion

The church-at-large has been a closed institution regarding its doctrine of the Trinity, which contains dogma that Jesus is God. But it is challenging for Trinitarians to have to prove their doctrine from the Bible. And this doctrine of the Trinity has proven through the centuries to be a serious hindrance for Christianity in its dialogue with other religions, especially with Judaism and Islam. I believe it is about time for the church to open its door to allow a more robust discussion about whether its doctrine of the Trinity, and thus that Jesus is God, can be supported from the Bible. The result may be that the church will experience a breath of fresh air.

Chapter 10
Restitution at the Judgment

Nicene church fathers, *you hit a bad shot* when you drafted your creed to say Jesus is God and all dissenters are condemned to hell! It took *a big divot* out of my life and the lives of many others. At the judgment, I think you will have to *replace the divot*.

"Avoid Stupid Controversies"

For twenty-eight years—from the time I began studying Jesus's identity until my book *The Restitution* was published—I kept my thoughts about this mostly to myself. I only shared them with a few close Christian friends. I had three reasons for this silence. First, it took me several years before I became certain what I believed about it. Second, I didn't want to cause controversy if I was uncertain. Third, I discovered that some of my friends had difficulty understanding what I was saying, or they seemed to purposely misrepresent it. So, I didn't want to go public about it until I had carefully written in a book what I was saying so that I couldn't be misunderstood or misrepresented.

Also, some of my Christian friends knew only that I no longer believed Jesus is God, yet they would avoid me without asking me about it. I decided that such rejection without inquiry paralleled something about Nicodemus. He was a Torah teacher and Sanhedrin member whom Jesus had told needed to be "born again" (John 3:1–21). It seems he became a secret believer in Jesus because he later entombed his deceased body (19:38–42). Earlier, when Nicodemus's religious associates tried to get Jesus arrested without questioning him, Nicodemus asked them, "Our law does not judge people without first giving them a hearing to find out what they are doing, does it?" (7:51).

Dietrich Bonhoeffer (1906-1945) was a German, Lutheran pastor, theologian, and anti-Nazi who was imprisoned during WWII and then executed. His book, *The Cost of Discipleship*, is a modern classic. Bonhoeffer states in his book, *Life Together*,

> The first service that one owes to others in the fellowship consists in listening to them. Just as love to God begins in listening to His Word, so the beginning of love for the brethren is learning to listen to them. It

is God's love for us that He not only gives us His Word but also lends us His ear. So it is His work that we do for our brother when we learn to listen to him. ... he who can no longer listen to his brother will soon be no longer listening to God.[62]

Another reason my Christian friends were avoiding me like the plague had to do with something the apostle Paul wrote to Titus. If they told their pastor about me, he might quote this text: "Have nothing more to do with anyone who causes divisions, since you know that such a person is perverted and sinful, being self-condemned" (Titus 3:10–11). But they would take it out of its context. This sentence begins, "After the first and second admonition," indicating they should have questioned me first. Moreover, Paul prefaces this remark by saying, "Avoid stupid controversies" (v. 9). He wrote likewise to Timothy, "Have nothing to do with stupid and senseless controversies; you know that they breed quarrels" (2 Timothy 2:23). So, what is a stupid controversy?

The "Arian controversy" that brought about the Nicene Council and its creed was *a very stupid controversy*! It was about whether the Logos had eternally preexisted, as Bishop Alexander insisted, or God created the Logos prior to creation, as Arius asserted. I think the bishop should have left this matter alone since it was unimportant. Scripture says nothing about it, making it a speculative matter. Recall that Moses wrote in the Torah, "The secret things belong to the LORD our God, but the revealed things"—which for us are in the Bible—"belong to us and to our children forever" (Deuteronomy 29:29). King David wrote, "O LORD, my heart is not lifted up, my eyes are not raised too high; I do not occupy myself with things too great and too marvelous for me" (Psalm 131:1).

Bishop Alexander was hostile in opposing Arius and thus defied Paul's warning, "The Lord's servant must not be quarrelsome but kindly to everyone, an apt teacher, patient, correcting opponents with gentleness" (2 Timothy 2:24–25). Paul explains that when believers engage in stupid controversies they get caught in "the snare of the devil, having been held captive by him to do his will" (v. 26). Such was the Nicene Council!

Paul wrote something else traditionalists might cite to justify avoiding people like me. He cautioned, "I urge you brothers and

---

[62] Dietrich Bonhoeffer, *Life Together*, tr. John W. Doberstein (New York: Harper & Row, 1954), 97–98.

sisters to keep an eye on those who cause dissensions and offenses, in opposition to the teaching that you have learned; avoid them" (Romans 16:17). But what was Paul's teaching? It did not expressly include that Jesus is God and God is three Persons. Rather, Gentile church fathers caused division when they departed from strict Jewish monotheism, which Paul taught and people like me try to restore. My Christology is much the same as that of Jewish Christians known as Nazarenes. If our Christology is correct, it is traditionalists who were schismatic.

Paul also taught, "Whoever teaches otherwise and does not agree with the sound words of our Lord Jesus Christ ... is conceited, understanding nothing, and has a morbid craving for controversy and for disputes about words" (1 Timothy 6:3–4). Guess what! There has never been a greater dispute about words in the history of the church, and maybe the history of the world, than the Nicene Council's dispute about two long Greek words that differed only with the letter "i" that were used to describe Jesus's identity.[63] It is worth quoting again historian Edward Gibbon's comment about this debacle: "The profane of every age have derided the furious contests which the difference of a single diphthong excited between the Homoousians and the Homoiousians."

Loving or Hating Our Brothers and Sisters in Christ

The main thing Jesus taught his apostles was that they *love one another*. At the Last Supper, after Judas Iscariot departed to betray Jesus, the Lord said to the Eleven, "I give you a new commandment, that you love one another. Just as I have loved you, you also should love one another" (John 13:34). How does this affect sharing the gospel? Many people claim that the most important Christian activity is spreading the gospel.

But it does us no good to share the gospel if we hate a spiritual brother or sister. Moreover, it is detrimental to the gospel! The apostle Paul indicated this in his letter to the Corinthians by saying, "If I speak in the tongues of mortals and of angels, but do not have love, I am a noisy gong or a clanging cymbal" (Romans 13:1).

The Bible calls upon believers to "love your neighbor as yourself" (Leviticus 19:18; Mark 12:31). Jesus added, "Love your enemies" (Matthew 5:44). But it seems so special that he told his apostles, "I give you a new commandment, that you love one another." He makes this so important. For he added, "By this everyone will know that you are

---

[63] It is *iota*, the ninth letter in the Greek alphabet. *Iota* is transliterated "i" in English.

my disciples, if you have love for one another" (John 13:35). So, if we do not love our brothers and sisters in Christ, our sharing of the gospel with the world will not only be in vain but detrimental. Yet, to love our brothers and sisters in Christ, we must know who they are. Therefore, we need to know what the Bible requires to be a Christian.

We have learned that the heart of the gospel is to believe that Jesus died for us and rose from the dead. We also saw in Chapter 5 that the Fourth Evangelist revealed his purpose for writing by saying, "These are written so that you may continue to believe that Jesus is the Messiah, the Son of God, and that through believing you may have life in his name" (John 20:31). Then 1 John echoes this by saying, "God abides in those who confess that Jesus is the Son of God" (1 John 4:15). It adds, "Everyone who believes that Jesus is the Christ has been born of God" (1 John 5:1). Therefore, believing Jesus is the Messiah/Christ, the Son of God, results in being born again and inheriting eternal life. As in John's gospel, 1 John does not require that we believe Jesus is God for salvation.

Yet, 1 John includes two solemn warnings about not loving our spiritual brothers and sisters who share this common faith. It warns, "Whoever does not love abides in death. All who hate a brother or sister are murderers, and you know that murderers do not have eternal life abiding in them" (1 John 3:14–15). It also says, "Those who say, 'I love God,' and hate a brother or sister are liars, for those who do not love a brother or sister, whom they have seen, cannot love God, whom they have not seen" (1 John 4:20).

The author of 1 John was writing about Docetists, a type of Gnostic who claimed Jesus did not have an actual physical body. That is why the author begins his epistle by affirming that Jesus came in the flesh. He says concerning Jesus that he and others of his church community "touched with our hands ... the word of life" (1 John 1:1).

Moreover, Jesus's teaching about judgment at the end of the age is most sobering regarding love (Matthew 25:31–46). He said of himself, "When the Son of Man comes in his glory, and all the angels with him, then he will sit on the throne of his glory. All the nations will be gathered before him, and he will separate people one from another as a shepherd separates the sheep from the goats" (vv. 31–32). Sheep symbolize the righteous who will "inherit the kingdom" and receive "eternal life," whereas goats symbolize the wicked. "The King" will say to them, "You that are accursed, depart from me into the eternal fire prepared for the devil and his angels" (vv. 34, 41). The basis for judgment is how both groups treated people who belonged to King Jesus, who seem to have been destitute and perhaps persecuted. To those who fed and clothed them, etc., Jesus will say to them, "Just as you did it to one of the least of these who are members of my family, you did it to me" (v. 40). Notice the expression, "members of my family."

Jesus spoke similarly in his Sermon on the Mount. He said of judgment day, "Not everyone who says to me 'Lord, Lord,' will enter the kingdom of heaven, but only the one who does the will of my Father in heaven. On that day many will say to me, 'Lord, Lord, did we not prophesy in your name, and cast out demons in your name, and do many deeds of power in your name?' Then I will declare to them, 'I never knew you; go away from me, you evildoers'" (Matthew 7:21–23).

Jesus also taught that our relationship with him depends on how much we love him. For he said, "If you love me, you will keep my commandments. ... They who have my commandments and keep them are those who love me; and those who love me will be loved by my Father, and I will love them and reveal myself to them" (John 14:15, 21). So the extent to which we obey Jesus's commandments will be reflected in our beliefs about him because they depend on how much he reveals himself to us.

Did Nicene fathers hate Arians and mistreat them? Yes. Yet Arians clearly were members of Jesus's family, thus their brothers and sisters. How so? Arians believed and confessed that Jesus is the Christ, the Son of God, that he died on the cross for their sins, and God raised him from the dead. The issue these two groups disputed—whether Jesus as the Logos-Son preexisted eternally and was equal to God, called "eternal generation," or he had an origin prior to creation—had nothing to do with salvation even though Nicene fathers claimed it did and put it in their creed.

Making Restitution at the Judgment

I titled my book, *The Restitution*, for two reasons. Foremost is that in it I seek to *restore* to Jesus his identity as a fully human being and thus not God. For many people, Jesus being God lessens his humanity. Roman Catholic Raymond E. Brown well states, "Many Christian believers do not sufficiently appreciate the humanity of Jesus."[64] And because of this, many scholars have alleged that the

---

[64] Brown, *Jesus God and Man*, ix.

teaching that Jesus is God has resulted somewhat in Christian belief in a docetic Christ.

Dictionaries explain that the word *restitution* has two meanings: restoration and reimbursement. So my secondary reason for *The Restitution* book title is that the misdeed of church fathers adding to the gospel that Jesus is God has caused believers like me to suffer loss. Thus, I think at the judgment church fathers and their followers who have caused such loss will have to *make restitution as a payback for causing this loss*. It will be like the Torah requiring restitution for stealing. Torah requires the thief to repay what was stolen plus one-fifth extra (Leviticus 6:1–5). Yet it also requires that some thieves be punished much more severely (Exodus 22:1).

What will King Jesus do at the judgment to those church fathers who changed his gospel without his approval? Will he do to them as in the parable of the talents that he taught (Matthew 25:14–30; Luke 19:12–27)? It is a story about a nobleman entrusting his possessions to his slaves, or servants, and then taking a journey. When he returned, he required an accounting from them. Those who invested their talents and made more were rewarded, but he who hid his talent, the nobleman took it and gave it to another.

Will it be that way at the judgment for Nicene fathers? Jesus entrusted them with his gospel. But they wrongfully added to it that he is God and condemned those who did not believe this. In doing so, they harmed their brothers and sisters who were faithful to the primitive gospel delivered by Jesus and his apostles and thus refused to accept this later addition. Nicene fathers and their followers condemned them as heretics and persecuted them. Being ostracized from church fellowship, some lost jobs, ministries, and much more. At the judgment, will Jesus then treat Nicene fathers like the servant in the parable who was untrustworthy with his master's possessions? That is, will Jesus take away rewards that were due Nicene fathers, and maybe some of those who followed them in their wrongful changing of the gospel, giving their rewards to those persecuted ones who had remained faithful to the Master's message? If so, such a restitution at the judgment will be payback for what was taken from them in this life.

Perhaps it is ironic that I related in *The Restitution* (p. 45) concerning the Nicene Council: "Roman Emperor Constantine gladly assembled the council with pomp, majesty, and eloquence. The large meetings were held in one of his magnificent and sumptuous palaces, called the Judgment Hall."

Conclusion

Nonetheless, church fathers, I will end this grievance against you by changing my tone. No one is perfect. Despite our shortcomings and sins, those of us who still served our Lord Jesus Christ faithfully will rejoice at the judgment if we hear him announce to us, "Come, you who are blessed by my Father, inherit the kingdom prepared for you from the foundation of the world" (Matthew 25:34). Hallelujah and Amen!

To all who confess Jesus Christ as risen Savior and heavenly-exalted Lord, let us unite in this confession and seek peace between us as brothers and sisters. I can extend the right hand of fellowship to all who so believe and make Jesus the Lord of their lives (Galatians 2:9). We should be able to love one another despite differences in other theological belief. Yet, if anyone asserts that I am *not* a Christian since I do not believe Jesus is God and God is three Persons, I cannot extend to that person the hand of Christian fellowship.

I now end this book by citing the end of my preface in *The Restitution* as follows: "I contend that the New Testament verifies that anyone who (1) truly believes Jesus is the Christ, the sinless Son of God, who died for their sins and arose bodily from the dead, and (2) confesses Him as Lord, manifesting evidence in their life to that effect, is indeed a genuine Christian believer and should be accepted as such."

[Dear reader, you scored a win by taking on this little book. Now you're ready to step up your game by tackling the big one—*The Restitution: Biblical Proof Jesus Is NOT God.*]

Works Cited

Akers, John N. et al., eds. *This We Believe: The Good News of Jesus Christ for the World*. Grand Rapids: Zondervan, 2000.
Bonhoeffer, Dietrich. *Life Together*. Tr. John W. Doberstein. New York: Harper & Row, 1954.
Brown, Raymond E. *Jesus God and Man: Modern Biblical Reflections*. New York: MacMillan, 1967.
——— . *An Introduction to New Testament Christology*. New York: Paulist, 1994.
Bultmann, Rudolf. *The Gospel of John: A Commentary*. Philadelphia: Westminster John Knox, 1971.
Dunn, James D. G. *Christology in the Making: A New Testament Inquiry Into the Origins of the Doctrine of the Incarnation*. Philadelphia: Westminster, 1980.
——— . *Did the First Christians Worship Jesus? The New Testament Evidence*. London: SPCK/Louisville: WJK, 2010.
Gibbon, Edward. *The History of the Decline and Fall of the Roman Empire*. 7 vols. London: Methuen, 1909.
Hanson, R.P.C. *The Search for the Christian Doctrine of God: The Arian Controversy, 318–381*. Orig. London: T.&T. Clark, 1988/Grand Rapids: Baker Academic, 2005.
Harnack, Adolf. *What Is Christianity?* Orig. 1900. Tr. T. B. Saunders. NY: Harper, 1957.
Harner, Philip B. "Qualitative Anarthrous Predicate Nouns: 15:39 and John 1.1." *Journal of Biblical Literature* 92 (1973): 75–87.
Hengel, Martin. *The Son of God: The Origin of Christology and the History of Jewish-Hellenistic Religion*. Orig. 1975. London: SCM/Philadelphia: Fortress, 1976.
——— . *Studies in Early Christology*. Edinburgh: T.&T. Clark, 1995.
Hurtado, Larry W. *One God, One Lord: Early Christian Devotion and Ancient Jewish Monotheism*. London: SCM, 1988.
Jenkins, Philip. *The Jesus Wars: How Four Patriarchs, Three Queens, and Two Emperors Decided What Christians Would Believe for the Next 1,500 Years*. New York: HarperCollins, 2010.
Klausner, Joseph. *The Messianic Idea in Israel: From Its Beginning to the Completion of the Mishnah*. Tr. W. F. Stinespring. New York: MacMillan, 1955.
Moule, C.F.D. *The Origin of Christology*. Cambridge: University, 1977.
Neusner, Jacob, and Bruce Chilton. *Jewish-Christian Debates: God, Kingdom, Messiah*. Minneapolis: Fortress, 1998.
Robinson, John A. T. *The Priority of John*. London: SCM, 1985/Oak Park, IL: Meyer-Stone, 1987.
Schaff, Philip. *History of the Christian Church*. 8 vols. 3rd ed. Orig. 1858. Rep. Grand Rapids: Eerdmans, 1985.
Wright, N. T. *Who Was Jesus?* London: SPCK/Grand Rapids: Eerdmans, 1992.
——— . *Jesus and the Victory of God*. Minneapolis: Fortress, 1996.
——— . *The Challenge of Jesus: Rediscovering Who Jesus Was and Is*. Downers Grove, IL: IVP, 1999.
Wright, N. T., and Marcus J. Borg. *The Meaning of Jesus: Two Visions*. New York: HarperCollins, 1999.
Young, F. "A Cloud of Witnesses" in John Hick, ed., *The Myth of God Incarnate*. Philadelphia: Westminster, 1977.
Zarley, Kermit. *The Gospels Interwoven*. Wheaton: Scripture Press, 1987.
——— . *The Restitution: Biblical Proof Jesus Is Not God*. 2008.

Author Index

Patristic Authors

Alexander of Alexandria, Bishop, 26–28, 44, 91
Arius of Alexandria, Presbyter, 10, 26–29, 44, 91
Athanasius of Alexandria, Bishop, 28–30
Basil of Caesarea, Bishop, 30–31
Eusebius of Caesarea, Bishop, 27
Gregory of Nazianzus, Bishop, 31
Gregory of Nyssa, Bishop, 31
Hippolytus of Rome, 25
Ignatius of Antioch, Bishop, 25
Origin of Alexandria, 25–27
Tertullian of Carthage, 25–26

Modern Authors

Alexander, Philip S., 77
Akers, John N., 85n56
Bonhoeffer, Dietrich, 90–91
Brown, Raymond E., 10, 38, 81, 94
Bultmann, Rudolf, 6–7
Chafer, Lewis Sperry, 4
Dunn, James D. G., 49, 62, 72, 77n45, 82, 83n54, 86–88
Gibbon, Edward, 27, 93
Hanson, R. P. C., 26–29, 80
Harnack, Adolf von, 80-81
Harner, Philip B., 6
Hengel, Martin, 44n29, 88
Hurtado, Larry W., 87–89
Jenkins, Philip, 33
Klausner, Joseph, 23
Moule, C. F. D., 81–82
Neusner, Jacob, 76
Newton, Sir Isaac, 29–30, 79
Robinson, John A.T., 47, 82
Schaff, Philip, 30
Wright, N. T., 87–89
Young, F., 79, 83
Zarley, Kermit, vii–viii, 10–11, 23, 25–26, 28, 33, 36, 47, 54, 62, 72–73, 79, 83, 85, 87, 89–90, 94–96

Subject and Name Index

A
Ackman, Bill, 11
Alexander of Alexandria, Bishop: death of, 28; denounces Arius' teaching, 26; first threatening letter of, 27; leader of orthodox party, 28
Alexandria, Egypt, 26
Allison Jr., Dale C., 8
Antioch, 25, 58
antisemitic, 76
apologists, definition of, 24–26, 82
Apostles Creed, the, 28, 32
Areopagus, 58, 65
Arius of Alexandria, Presbyter, 19, 26–28, 44, 91
Arian Controversy, 28, 44, 80, 91
Athanasius of Alexandria, Bishop, 28–30

B
baptism, 39.
Basil the Great of Caesarea, Bishop, 31
Bebbington, David W., 84
Bebbington/Evangelical Quadrilateral, the, 84
born again/new birth, 2, 12, 18, 45–46, 48, 90–91
Bright, Bill, 85
Brown, Raymond E., 10, 38, 81, 94

C
Caesarea Philippi, 37
Cappadocians, the three, 30
Carson, D. A., 85
Chalcedonian Definition of Faith, vii, 31–32
Christ (also see Jesus): deity/divinity of, viii, 3, 23, 28, 42, 67, 79, 84–86; hypostatic union of, 2–3, 32, 80; incarnation of, vii, 32, 39, 47, 55, 65, 74, 76–77; preexisted/preexistence of, 3–4, 7, 25–26, 33–34, 39, 42, 64, 74, 94

Christadelphians, 85
Christology: Agent, 47–48, 52–53; Christ-is-God, 89; God-in-Christ, 89; high, 82–83; low, 82; riddle of, 44; Sending, 47–48
church fathers, categorizing of, 24
Clement of Alexandria, Egypt, 25
Clowney, Ed, 5
Colson, Charles, 85
Copernicus, 32
Council of Chalcedon (451), vii, 31, 33
Council of Constantinople (381), 30–32
Council of Nicaea (325), 25
critical thinking, 38
Cullmann, Oscar, 81

D
Dallas Theological Seminary, 2n3, 4–5
Deism, 30
Docetism/Docetist/Docetic, 44, 69, 77, 83, 93
Dodd, C. H., 82
Dunn, James D. G., 49, 62, 72, 82, 86–88

E
Ebionites (also see Jewish Christians), 75
ecumenical councils, 2, 10, 24, 31, 33–34
eternal generation, 26–27, 39, 94
Eucharist/communion service, 39–40
evangelicalism, beginning and definition of, 84

F
Falwell, Jerry, 85
Fellowship, The, 5
First Jewish Revolt, 76

G
Galileo, 32–33
Gnosticism/Gnostic, 44, 93

Gnostic Redeemer Myth, 42
gospel (Gr. *euangelion*), the: adding to, 12, 20, 34, 63, 70, 73, 86, 95; core elements of, 24, 67; meaning of, 14–16; simplicity of, 22–23
gospel, a different, 21–22, 68–69, 73
Graham, Billy, 19–20, 32, 83, 85
grammatical difficulties, 12, 71–72
Gregory of Nazianzus, 31
Gregory of Nyssa, Bishop, 31

H
Hahn, Ferdinand, 81
Harnack, Adolf von, 80
Harner, Philip, 6
Hillel, school of, 9
Hippolytus of Rome, 25
Hiskey, Babe, 5
Hiskey, Jim, 5
homoiousios/Homoiousians, 27, 92
homoousios/Homoousians, 27, 92
Houston, James, 5
Hunn, Marvin, 6

I
Ignatius of Antioch, Bishop, 25
incarnation, definition of, 55, 74
International Congress on World Evangelism, 83
Irenaeus of Lyons, Bishop, 25
Irwin, Hale, 4

J
Jefferson, Thomas, 30
Jehovah Witnesses, 21
Jesus (also see Christ): another, 21–22, 68–69, 73; meaning of, 45; overcomer, the, 51–52; virgin birth of, 19, 40–41, 75, 77
Jesus movement, early, 54, 75
Jesus-olatry, the danger of, 87
Jewish Christians, early, 75–76, 91
Johnson Jr., S. Lewis, 5–6, 32,
Judaizers, 69, 73
Justin Martyr of Rome, 25

K
Kermit Zarley Blog, 1n1
kingdom of God, how to enter the, 18, 35, 49, 93

L
Lausanne Covenant, the, 83
Lausanne Movement, the, 83
Legonier Ministries/Conference Center, vii, 5
LifeWay Research, 84
Locke, John, 3
Logos-Son, definition of the, 25–26, 94
logos speculation, 33–34

M
Manichaeans, 42
Martyr, Justin, 25
McKnight, Scot, 76n43, 82
minim/heretics, 76
monotheism, 26, 71, 74, 91
Mormons, 21
Mosher Library, 6
Moule, C. F. D., 81-82
Muhammad (Eng. Mohammed), 7
mutual indwelling, the, 7, 52

N
National Association of Evangelicals in the US (NAE), 84
Nazarenes (also see Jewish Christians), 75–76, 91
Nebuchadnezzar, King of Babylon, 15
new covenant, 46, 67
new perspective on Paul, 49
Newton, Sir Isaac, 29–30, 79
Nicene-Constantinopolitan Creed, the, 31
Nicene Creed, the, 1, 10, 27–28, 30–31, 34
Nicklaus, Jack, 4, 20

O
Oneness Pentecostals, 83, 85
Origen of Alexandria, 25–26

Subject and Name Index

P
Packer, J. I., 85
Palmer, Arnold, 5
Pebble Beach Golf Course, 4
PGA Tour Bible Study, 12, 20

Q
Quest for the historical Jesus, the, 88

R
Regents College, 5
restitution, meaning of, 94–95
Robertson, Pat, 85
Roman emperors: Constantine, 10, 25, 95: Theodosius, 31
Rome, 31, 60, 66, 76

S
Schweitzer, Albert, 80
Second Jewish Revolt, 76
Shammai, school of, 9
Shema, the, 71, 74
Sproul, R. C., vii, 5, 85
Stott, John, 85
Strange, Curtis, 4
Supersessionism/Replacement Theory, 76
Swindoll, Charles, 85

T
Tertullian of Carthage, 25
theosis, 30, 30n18
Theotokos (mother of God), vii, 31–32
traditionalist, definition of, 8
Trevino, Lee, 12
Trinitarianism, 6, 84
Trinity, doctrine of the, 2, 11, 21, 23, 30–31, 77, 85, 89
tritheism, 31
twelve apostles, choosing of, 9, 23, 37, 68, 73

U
U. S. Open Golf Championship, 4

W
Walvoord, John, 85
Weiskopf, Tom, 4
Westminster Theological Seminary, 5
Woodbridge, John, 85

Y
Yakima Firing Range, 85

Z
Zarley Lectures, 82, 88

Scripture Index

Old Testament

Exodus
4:22	40
22:1	95

Leviticus
6:1–5	95
19:18	92

Numbers
21:9	47
23:9	37

Deuteronomy
4:2	34
6:4	71, 74
10:16	18, 46
29:29	33, 91
30:6	18

2 Samuel
7:12–15	78
7:14	40

1 Kings
11:1	78
11:3–4	78

1 Chronicles
17:13	40

Job
1—2	40

Psalms
2:2	41
2:7	41
16:10	56, 68
22	68
82:6	87
109:8	55
131:1	33, 91

Proverbs
30:5–6	34

Ecclesiastes
4:4	21
5:2	32
6:11	32
7:8	78

Isaiah
40:1–11	15
40:9	15
40:9–10	14
49:4–5	51
52:7	15–16
52:7–10	15
52:10	15
52:13—53:12	68
53	15
53:1	15–16
53:7	12
61:1	17, 51
61:1–2	15

Jeremiah
4:4	18
31:31	46
31:33	46

Ezekiel
36:25–26	18
36:25–29	46

Daniel
2	15
7:13–14	15, 43, 51

Hosea
11:1	40

Micah
5:2	51
5:4	51

New Testament

Matthew
1:18–25	19
3:2	35
3:17	40–41
4:1–11	41
4:3	41
4:6	41
4:11	52
4:17	35
4:23	17
5:3–10	49
5:9	40, 79
5:20	49
5:44	92
5:45	40
7:1–5	38
7:7	9
7:7–8	38
7:15–16	30
7:21–23	94
7:23	49
9:1–8	42
9:35	17
10:5	18
10:7	18
11:25–27	39
15:24	18
16:13	37
16:13–16	37
16:15–17	37
16:16	41
16:17	41
16:21	48
16:31	36
17:22–23	48
17:23	36
20:18–19	36, 48
24—25	2
24:36	2, 9
25:14–30	95
25:31–32	93
25:31–46	93

Scripture Index

25:34	93, 95	18:31–33	48	10:7	36
25:40	93	19:12–27	95	10:30	3
25:41	93	20:36	40	10:30–38	48
26:26–28	39	22:1–20	39	10:33	41
26:26–29	39	24:26	36	10:33–34	49
26:57–68	41	24:46–47	36	10:33–35	87
26:63	41			10:36	49

John

				10:38	52
Mark		1:1	72, 81, 86	11:25	50
1:1	16, 35	1:1c	3, 6, 8, 38	11:27	50
1:11	40	1:1c	50, 72, 82	12:13–15	50
1:12–13	41	1:12	45	12:32	47
1:14–15	16, 35	1:14	6, 33, 82, 86	12:34	50
2:1–12	42	1:18	8, 72	12:42-43	10
2:5	42	1:45	37	13:34	92
2:7	42	1:49	37	13:35	92
2:10	42	3:1–3	46	14:5–11	7
8:27–29	37	3:1–21	90	14:6	36, 71, 75
8:31	48	3:3	18	14:8–9	7
9:31	48	3:14	18, 46	14:10–11	7, 52
10:33–34	48	3:16	18	14:15	94
12:31	92	3:16-18	19	14:21	94
14:22–25	39	3:18	45	14:28	52
14:53–65	41	3:36	18	17:1–3	53
		4:25–26	50	17:6	45
Luke		5:1–16	48	17:11–12	45
1:2–3	62	5:17	48	17:26	45
1:19	16	5:18	41, 48	19:38–42	90
1:26–35	19	5:18–47	48	20:17	51
1:31–33	16	5:19	48, 56	20:28	3, 6–8, 38
8:281:32	40	5:19–47	48	20:28	51–52, 72, 81
1:35	40–41	5:24	47	20:30–31	50
1:51	14	5:26–27	42	20:31	93
2:10	16	5:27	43	21	50
2:10–11	17	5:29	48		
3:22	40	5:30	48, 56	**Acts**	
4:1–13	41	5:43	45	1:1–2	54
4:18	17	5:44	53	1:2	54
4:21	17	6	7	1:3	54
4:41	41	6:29	47	1:4–8	55
5:17–26	42	6:41	7	1:9	55
6:35	40	6:53	7	1:9–11	54
8:28	40	7:26	50	1:11	55
9:18–20	37	7:31	50	1:13	55
9:22	48	7:41–43	50	1:15	55
9:44	48	7:51	90	1:16–20	55
10:21–22	39	8:25	50	1:20	55
11:20	36	8:53	50	1:21–22	55
17:21	36	9:22	50	1:26	55

2:22–24	56	17:18	58	8:14	40
2:27	56	17:19	58	8:19	40
2:27–32	68	17:22–31	65	9:5	8, 21, 66, 72
2:31	56	17:24	59	10:9–10	22, 66
3:13	56	17:30–31	66	10:15–16	16
3:15	56, 62	17:31–34	59	11:13	64
3:19	56	18:1	59, 64, 67	13:1	92
4:2	56	18:4–5	59	15:6	70
4:10–11	56	18:5	64	15:19	66
4:13	9	18:24	59	16:17	91
4:33	56	18:28	59	16:25	64
5:17–18	56	19:1	59	16:26	66
5:27	56	19:4–5	59	16:26–27	16:26–27
5:29–32	56	19:8	59		
5:41–42	56	19:9	75	**1 Corinthians**	
6:5	54	19:23	75	1:11–13	67
7:2–53	54, 56	20:18	59	1:17	67
7:51	46, 57	20:20–21	59	1:21	67
7:55–58	57	20:25	59	1:23	67
8:1	57	20:28	59	2:1–2	67
8:4–40	54	22:4	75	6:9–11	49
8:5	57	22:6	59	8:4	71
8:12	57	24:5	75	8:5–6	30
8:25	57	24:10	60	8:6	71
8:27	57	24:14	75	11:20	39
8:31	57	24:14–17	60	11:23–26	39, 67
8:35	57	24:20–21	60	15:1–4	22
9:2	75	24:22	76	15:1–5	67
9:19–20	57	25:19	60	15:3–4	68
9:22	57	25:22	60	15:3–5	19
10:38–41	58	26:1–3	60		
11:20	56	26:6–8	60	**2 Corinthians**	
13:23	58	26:19–23	60	1:3	70
13:28–33	58	28:16–17	61	10:1	12
13:34–37	68	28:19–23	61	10:5	73
13:35	58			10:5–6	12
15	24, 73	**Romans**		11:3–4	22–23, 69
16:25	65	1:1–4	66	11:4	69
16:26	58	1:6	66	11:13	68
16:29–31	58	1:7–8	70	11:31	70
16:30–31	65	1:15	66		
17:1–3	58, 65	1:16	66	**Galatians**	
17:2–3	61	1:17	49	1:3–4	69
17:6	61	2:6–10	49	1:6–9	22, 69
17:6–7	65	2:16	64	1:8–9	64
17:10	65	3:20	49	1:11–12	68
17:11	65	3:28	49	2:1–2	68
17:13–15	65	3:30	70	2:2	73
17:16–18	58	6:3–4	39	2:7–9	68

Scripture Index

2:7–10	73	2:13	8, 21, 66, 72	16:7	52
2:9	96	3:9	91	16:14	52
3:20	69	3:10–11	91	19:6	52
3:26	40			19:15	52
5:4	69	**Hebrews**		20:11–12	49
5:19–21	49	1:3	86	21:22	52
		1:8	8, 38, 72, 81		

Ephesians

1:3	70
1:13	19
1:17	70
2:8	19
4:3	21
4:6	71
5:5–6	49

Philippians

2:5–11	72
2:6–7	72

Colossians

1:3	70
2:12	39
4:14	54

2 Thessalonians

1:12	8, 21, 66, 72

1 Timothy

1:17	42, 71
2:5–6	71
5:1	29
6:3–4	92
6:15–16	71
6:16	42

2 Timothy

1:13	69
1:14	70
2:2	70
2:8	64, 70
2:23	91
2:24–25	91
2:26	91
3:16	10, 23
4:11	54

Titus

1:16	49

Hebrews

2:17	42–43
9:27	36

James

1:13	52
2:24	49
2:26	49

1 Peter

1:19	52
2:21	13

2 Peter

1:1	8, 72
1:4	30

1 John

1:1	93
2:2	50
2:3–4	48
2:29	48
3:1	48
3:14–15	93
4:10	50
4:15	93
4:20	93
5:1	93
5:20	8, 72

Jude

3	80
3–4	22
4	70

Revelation

1:8	52
2--3	51
3:12	51
3:21	51
4:8	52
11:17	52
15:3	52

Other Religious Literature

Qur'an
3:57	77
3:63	77
4:71-72	77
4:15	77
5:16	77
5:72	77
5:72-73	79
5:73	77
5:75	77
5:116	77
9:30-31	77
19:20-21	77

The Real Jesus

Jesus of Nazareth is the most famous man who has ever lived. But who was he? To learn about his identity, we must turn to the Bible. The New Testament presents Jesus as a seer-prophet, a teaching rabbi, an itinerant preacher, a wisdom sage, a charismatic healer, a miracle worker, and an exorcist. It applies to him the titles Messiah/Christ, Son of Man, Son of God, Savior, and Lord. It says he was born of a virgin, lived a sinless life in obedience to God, and died on a cross due to sinful men. Yet Jesus' suffering and death was according to God's plan as atonement for the sins of others. For those who believe these things about Jesus, God will forgive them of their sins and give them eternal life.

The New Testament also proclaims that God vindicated Jesus by literally raising him from the dead. It reveals that for the next forty days Jesus literally appeared to many of his disciples on multiple occasions, after which he ascended from their midst into heaven. Then God exalted Jesus by inviting him to sit with him on his throne. The New Testament also reveals that Jesus will dramatically return to the earth sometime in the future, bringing with him his promised and glorious kingdom. Then God will bring about the resurrection of the dead as well as judgment day.

During the early centuries of Christianity, the Catholic Church adhered faithfully to these scriptural teachings about Jesus. But in the fourth and fifth centuries, it officially proclaimed that Jesus was not only a man but also God by possessing two natures: a fully human nature and a fully divine nature, the latter called "the deity of Christ." And through the Church's councils and creeds it pronounced that if anyone did not believe that Jesus was fully God—co-equal and co-eternal with God the Father and the Holy Spirit—that person did not really believe in Jesus and thus was not a genuine Christian. Roman Catholic, Greek Orthodox, and Protestant church denominations still officially embrace these additional proclamations, claiming that they reflect the New Testament. And these churches identify the Father, Son, and Spirit as a "Trinity" even though this word is not in the Bible.

When the Catholic Church identified Jesus as "God," it departed from the fundamental, biblical, Judeo-Christian teaching that God is "one," later called "monotheism." It happened because, when the Church expanded into Gentile lands, it gradually (1) became rather anti-Semitic, (2) abandoned the established principle of using only biblical terms and categories with which to identify Jesus, (3) went beyond Scripture by introducing Greek metaphysics into theology in an effort to identify Jesus more precisely, and therefore (4) interpreted Jesus' status as "the Son of God" ontologically, thereby making this title synonymous with the word "God." Instead, Jesus should be understood as the Son of God in a Jewish context, so that this title means One specially favored by God to be Israel's Messiah.

Jesus was not God because of the following biblical evidence or lack thereof:
There is *no* New Testament evidence that Jesus ever *thought* that he was God.
There is *no* New Testament evidence that Jesus ever *claimed* that he was God.
There *is* New Testament evidence that Jesus *denied* that he claimed to be God.
At Jesus' examination before the Sanhedrin, he was *never* accused of ever claiming to be God.
The New Testament regularly *distinguishes* between God and Jesus as two separate individuals.
The New Testament constantly *interchanges* the words "God" and "the Father."
The New Testament repeatedly identifies "God" *exclusively* as "the Father."
The New Testament contains *no* unambiguous statement such as "Jesus (Christ) is God."
In the synoptic gospels and evangelistic sermons in Acts, Jesus is *never* identified as "God."

Jesus was not God because Jesus said of himself:
"Why do you call me good? No one is good but God alone" (Mark 10:18).1
"The Son can do nothing on his own but only what he sees the Father doing" (John 5:19, cf. v. 30).
"You" are "making yourself God." Jesus replied, "I said, 'I am God's Son'" (John 10:33, 36).
"The Father is greater than I" (John 14:28).
Jesus prayed, "Father,... the only true God, and Jesus Christ whom you have sent" (John 17:1, 3).
"Jesus said to her,... 'I am ascending to my Father ... to my God and your God'" (John 20:17).

Jesus was not God because of the following additional Scriptures:
Jesus was visible, but God is "invisible" to humans (1 John 1:1-3; 1:18; 1 Timothy 1:17).
Jesus was approachable, but God "dwells in unapproachable light" (1 Timothy 6:16; cf. Psalm 104:2).
Jesus was tempted, but "God cannot be tempted by evil" (Mark 1:13; James 1:13).
Jesus was mortal, dying on a cross, so that "only God" is "immortal" (1 Timothy 1:17; 6:16).
Jesus said the Father is "the one who alone is God" and "the only true God" (John 5:44; 17:3).
Jesus called the Father "my God" several times (Matthew 27:46; John 20:17; Revelation 3:2, 12).
Paul wrote that "God is one" and "the only wise God" (Romans 3:30; 16:27).
Paul wrote that the Father is "the only God" and "only Sovereign" (1Timothy 1:17; 6:15).

Peter did not believe Jesus was God since he distinguished them as follows:
"Jesus of Nazareth, a man attested to you by God with deeds of power, wonders, and signs that God did through him among you" (Acts 2:22).
"Rulers of the people and elders,... Jesus Christ of Nazareth, whom you crucified, whom God raised from the dead" (Acts 4:8, 10).
"God has made him both Lord and Messiah, this Jesus whom you crucified" (Acts 2:36).
"God anointed Jesus of Nazareth with the Holy Spirit and with power;... he went about doing good and healing all who were oppressed by the devil, for God was with him" (Acts 10:38).

Paul the monotheist did not believe Jesus was God because he wrote the following:
"For there is one God; there is also one mediator between God and humankind, Christ Jesus, himself human" (1 Timothy 2:5).
"There is no God but one.... there is one God, the Father, from whom are all things and for whom we exist, and one Lord, Jesus Christ, through whom are all things and through whom we exist" (1 Corinthians 8:4, 6).
"There is ... one Lord, one faith, one baptism, one God and Father" (Ephesians 4:4-6).
"God and Father of our/the Lord Jesus" (Romans 15.6; 2 Corinthians 1:3; 11:31; Ephesians 1:3, 17).
"Christ is God's" because "God is the head of Christ" (1 Corinthians 3:23; 11:3).
"In Christ God was reconciling the world to himself" (2 Corinthians 5:19).
"Grace to you and peace from God our Father and the Lord Jesus Christ" (salutations 6x).

Jesus was not God because of the following logical reasons:
If Jesus did miracles by means of a divine nature, the Father *did not* do the works of Jesus.
If Jesus' ability to do miracles was intrinsic, he did *not need* the power of the Holy Spirit.
God is totally self-sufficient, but Jesus *needed* the miracle-working power of God's Spirit.
There is *no* biblical evidence that Jesus had two natures and two wills, which is non-human.
God transcends his creation, so that being God is *incompatible* with being human.
God foreknew the yet future date of Jesus' return to earth, but Jesus *did not* know it (Mark 13:32).

Thus, the New Testament *does not* teach Jesus was God, but that God *sent* him,2 God was *with* him,3 God was *in* him,4 and God *raised* Jesus from the dead. The traditional view that Jesus is God is based on only a few Bible texts.5 Most of them have grammatical difficulties partly due to the primitive structure of ancient language. Thus, Bible versions often differ as to whether they call Jesus "God." Some texts are rightly interpreted to mean, *God was in Christ*, not Christ was God. In sum, Jesus was not God but a virgin-born man who endured temptation, suffering, shame, trial, and violent execution to provide salvation for us, and God vindicated and exalted him for it. Praise Jesus and his God!

Kermit Zarley wrote this tract as a condensation of his (now retitled) book, *The Restitution: Biblical Proof Jesus Is Not God*. Visit his website, kermitzarley.com, to print this tract free and learn about him and his several books on biblical studies that are available on amazon.com. Mr. Zarley is known mostly for his lifetime career as a pro golfer on the PGA Tour and its Champions Tour. He was a pioneer in bringing Christianity to American professional sports by co-founding and leading the PGA Tour Bible Study, which still thrives today. Kermit also has been a member of the Society of Biblical Literature since 1999.

1 All Bible references are from the New Revised Standard Version, Updated Edition (NRSVue).
2 It is stated over forty times in the Gospel of John that God "sent," or did "send," Jesus.
3 John 3:2; 8:29; 16:32; Acts 10:38; cf. John 1:1-2.
4 John 10:38; 14:10-11; 17:21; 2 Corinthians 5:19.
5 The most prominent are the following: Isaiah 9:6; John 1:1, 18; 10:30; 20:28; Romans 9:5; Philippians 2:6-7; 2 Thessalonians 1:12; Titus 2:13; Hebrews 1:8; 2 Peter 1:1; 1 John 5:20.

Still Here Books
on Bible Prophecy by Kermit Zarley

ISBN: 978-1-933538-43-3

ISBN: 978-0-9815462-2-3

ISBN: 978-1-7352591-0-9

ISBN: 978-1-7352591-2-3

★★★★★
Leave Kermit a review at Amazon.com!

Go to https://amazon.com and search for "Kermit Zarley Books"
Select a book you have read, scroll down and click on "Write a Customer Review"
Write your review... and THANK YOU!

Other Books
by Kermit Zarley

ISBN: 978-1-55635-181-5

ISBN: 978-1-57910-775-8

ISBN: 978-1-7352591-6-1

ISBN: 978-1-4982-2528-1

★★★★★
Leave Kermit a review at Amazon.com!

Go to https://amazon.com and search for "Kermit Zarley Books"
Select a book you have read, scroll down and click on "Write a Customer Review"
Write your review... and THANK YOU!

Printed in Great Britain
by Amazon